UNCERTAINTY X DESIGN

Realizing more promising futures starts in the *here-and-now*. This book prepares young people to become the creative authors of their own lives by teaching them to approach current and future uncertainties with an unshakable sense of possibility. It explains how students can benefit from opportunities to take creative action when facing uncertainty *by design*. The book introduces a framework for educators, researchers, and parents to understand, develop, and examine learning experiences aimed at helping young people unleash their creative potential, both now and into the future.

RONALD A. BEGHETTO is an internationally recognized expert on creative thought and action in educational settings. He holds the Pinnacle West Presidential Chair at Arizona State University, USA, and is a Fellow of the American Psychological Association. He has been named one of the Top 200 University-Based Scholars in Education by *Education Week*.

UNCERTAINTY X DESIGN

Educating for Possible Futures

RONALD A. BEGHETTO
Arizona State University

Shaftesbury Road, Cambridge CB2 8EA, United Kingdom

One Liberty Plaza, 20th Floor, New York, NY 10006, USA

477 Williamstown Road, Port Melbourne, VIC 3207, Australia

314–321, 3rd Floor, Plot 3, Splendor Forum, Jasola District Centre, New Delhi – 110025, India

103 Penang Road, #05–06/07, Visioncrest Commercial, Singapore 238467

Cambridge University Press is part of Cambridge University Press & Assessment, a department of the University of Cambridge.

We share the University's mission to contribute to society through the pursuit of education, learning and research at the highest international levels of excellence.

www.cambridge.org
Information on this title: www.cambridge.org/9781009069854

DOI: 10.1017/9781009071475

© Ronald A. Beghetto 2024

This publication is in copyright. Subject to statutory exception and to the provisions of relevant collective licensing agreements, no reproduction of any part may take place without the written permission of Cambridge University Press & Assessment.

First published 2024
First paperback edition 2024

A catalogue record for this publication is available from the British Library

Library of Congress Cataloging-in-Publication data
NAMES: Beghetto, Ronald A., 1969– author.
TITLE: Uncertainty x design : educating for possible futures / Ronald A. Beghetto.
DESCRIPTION: Cambridge, United Kingdom ; New York, NY : Cambridge University Press, 2023. | Includes bibliographical references and index.
IDENTIFIERS: LCCN 2023021423 (print) | LCCN 2023021424 (ebook) | ISBN 9781316512968 (hardback) | ISBN 9781009069854 (paperback) | ISBN 9781009071475 (epub)
SUBJECTS: LCSH: Creative teaching. | Creative thinking–Study and teaching. | Uncertainty.
CLASSIFICATION: LCC LB1025.3 .B4474 2023 (print) | LCC LB1025.3 (ebook) | DDC 371.102–dc23/eng/20230602
LC record available at https://lccn.loc.gov/2023021423
LC ebook record available at https://lccn.loc.gov/2023021424

ISBN 978-1-316-51296-8 Hardback
ISBN 978-1-009-06985-4 Paperback

Cambridge University Press & Assessment has no responsibility for the persistence or accuracy of URLs for external or third-party internet websites referred to in this publication and does not guarantee that any content on such websites is, or will remain, accurate or appropriate.

*For Olivia and all young people,
may you always see the possible
in the uncertainty you face now
and into your futures.*

Contents

List of Figures	*page* ix
Preface	xi
Acknowledgments	xvi

PART I APPROACHING UNCERTAIN FUTURES

1 What Do We Owe Students?   3
    Application 1   Exploring Possible Educational Futures   12
    Application 1.1   Educational Futures Protocol   12
    Application 1.2   Walk-Through: Educational Futures Protocol   14

2 Designing for Likely Futures   19
    Application 2   Moving from Mitigating toward Embracing Uncertainty   32
    Application 2.1   Example and Analysis of the Logic of Backward Design   32
    Application 2.2   Embracing Uncertainty to Promote Generative Learning   37

3 Designing for Uncertain Futures   40
    Application 3   Embracing the Uncertainty of Blended Designs   49
    Application 3.1   Protocol for Exploring Blended Designs   49
    Application 3.2   Example Walk-Through of the Protocol   50

4 Start with Uncertainty   54
    Application 4   Exploring Teacher-Student Knowns and Unknowns   67
    Application 4.1   Protocol for Exploring Knowns and Unknowns   67
    Application 4.2   Example Walk-Through of the Protocol   69

viii *Contents*

PART II DESIGNING FOR UNCERTAIN FUTURES

5 Structuring Uncertainty for Learning   77
    Application 5   Hybrid Lessons and UxD Project Examples 90
    Application 5.1 Examples of Hybrid Lessons 90
    Application 5.2 UxD "Starter" Examples 93

6 Seeing the Possible in Uncertainty   96
    Application 6   Producing and Pre-testing Possibilities 109
    Application 6.1 Protocol for Producing and Pre-testing Possibilities 109
    Application 6.2 Example Walk-Through of the Protocol 111

7 To Act or Not to Act   115
    Application 7   Monitoring and Supporting Students' Agentic Beliefs 131
    Application 7.1 UxD Pre-checks and Initial Supports 131
    Application 7.2 UxD Check-ins and Timely Supports 133
    Application 7.3 UxD Post-checks and Reflective Supports 135

8 Making Principled Contributions   138
    Application 8   How Can We Ensure That Our Work Is Benefiting Others? 156
    Application 8.1 UxD Planning and Impact Monitoring Template 156
    Application 8.2 Example of UxD Planning and Impact Monitoring 156
    Application 8.3 Post-project Reflection Template 158
    Application 8.4 Example of Post-project Reflection 158

Avanti From What Is to What Could Be   160

References 162
Index 173

Figures

1.1	Possible trajectories from likely to unknown futures	*page* 6
2.1	Model of backward design	22
2.2	Olivia playing school	25
2.3	Open and closed moments across the interaction	35
3.1	Model of the UxD approach	44
4.1	Experiences of uncertainty by intensity and duration	60
4.2	Dimensions of teacher-student knowing and unknowing	65
5.1	Structured uncertainty and the continuum of possible learning experiences	79
5.2	Picasso's Bull series lithographs	82
6.1	Making the familiar unfamiliar and the unfamiliar familiar	101
6.2	Selecting, refining, and reidentifying actionable possibilities	104
7.1	Thresholds of action under uncertainty	117
8.1	Cone of contributions	144
8.2	Types of generative and principled reasoning in UxD	154

Preface

It's a feature, not a bug.

—Unknown Origin[1]

Uncertainty is a "feature" of learning and life, not a "bug" in the system. This book is about helping young people learn how to approach the uncertainty they face with an unshakable sense of the possible. More specifically, this book describes how students can benefit from opportunities to take creative action in the face of uncertainty *by design*. In this way, this book serves as a prolonged exercise in possibility thinking – providing insights, scenarios, and applications for educators and researchers committed to supporting young people in embracing uncertainty and becoming the creative authors of their own futures.

Although this book is aimed at educators, educational designers, students of education, and researchers, it is relevant for anyone interested in exploring new possibilities for designing educational learning experiences. This book can help support and structure possibility thinking for individuals and groups, including parents wondering what might be possible for their own children.

In fact, parents often turn to education with the hope that it will equip their children to not only learn academic subject matter but also be able to put their learning and unique talents to creative use – benefitting their own lives and the world around them. Consider, for instance, the following conversation between two parents who will soon be sending their children to school:

---

[1] This is a common phrase used in computer science and technology. Although the precise origin of the phrase is unknown, its popularity has been attributed to Grace Hopper (1906–1992), an early pioneer in the field of computer science, who worked on the Harvard Mark II computer. A problem in the system was traced to a bug (i.e., a moth) trapped between the relay contacts in the computer. The bug was removed and taped by Hopper to the logbook, which serves as the basis of errors in computing being called "bugs" (www.computerhistory.org/tdih/september/9/).

PARENT 1: I can't believe it's already time to send our kids off to school! They grow up so fast.

PARENT 2: Yeah, I know what you mean – they just seem to get bigger and smarter each day. It seems like only yesterday we were bringing them home from the hospital! What do you hope for your child this year?

PARENT 1: I'm feeling excited and anxious – a bit nervous too! Of course, I just want them to do well academically. But also, more importantly, that they find joy in learning! What about you?

PARENT 2: Absolutely – academics are important for their future success but really what's most essential is the development of creativity, critical thinking skills, and resilience. We need to provide them with an education that will prepare them for a future of uncertainty.

PARENT 1: That's true! Education should be more than just memorizing facts and formulas – we must think bigger and bolder when it comes to preparing our children for their futures. It needs to become dynamic, so they can access knowledge in multiple ways on the go or through digital resources such as podcasts or videos – all while creating meaningful connections within the classroom setting itself.

PARENT 2: Absolutely, and there are many innovative tools available to teachers these days that make it easier for them to provide a well-rounded education. We need to focus on creating an environment where students can be active participants in their own learning – not just passive recipients of information. We also have to think about how technology can be used ethically and responsibly.

PARENT 1: That's a great point – we need to make sure that our kids are learning the skills necessary for them not just to survive but really thrive in an ever-changing world. What if, instead of "teaching" students traditional subject matter, schools become more like incubators where students practice problem-solving and experimentation?

PARENT 2: Absolutely! Schools should encourage exploration and risk-taking so that their future is much brighter than ours! And I believe it won't take long before such educational paradigms start playing out on a large scale within classrooms across the globe …

PARENT 1: You're right, and it's something we should explore further. We need to bring together parents, educators, students – everyone who has a vested interest in this conversation – so that we can begin to map out our visions of education for the future!

PARENT 2: That's a great idea! We should arrange a meeting and get the ball rolling. I need to head off for work now, but we can touch base soon to discuss further.

PARENT 1: Sounds good – talk soon!

As illustrated in the above conversation, parents often think and even worry about the educational experiences their children will encounter. The good news is the kinds of possibilities mentioned in the example are certainly within reach. Moreover, there are potentially even more promising possibilities yet to be discovered. This is not intended to downplay parents' doubts or concerns. Instead, exploring the realm of possibility is not simply an exercise in cold logic; it often involves a range of emotions.

Although engaging with uncertainty can be an uncomfortable experience, this book invites us to step boldly into the uncertainty surrounding how we might better prepare young people to navigate the unknowns they encounter in their own learning and lives. Indeed, we all have a vested interest and shared responsibility to provide young people with meaningful educational experiences. That interest becomes activated whenever we face the increased uncertainty of a rapidly changing world.

When we face the unknown, we find ourselves at a crossroads. We can choose a path aimed at avoiding, downplaying, or minimizing uncertainty. Or we can choose to approach that uncertainty with a spirit of the possible. Doing so requires a blend of both imaginative and principled thinking to generate new and promising possibilities and, of course, the willingness to act on those possibilities.

Rapid advances in technology serve as an instructive example of how quickly change can be upon us and propel us into considering new possibilities for how we approach education now and into the future. In fact, the above conversation between parents was not written by me (the author of this book), but rather by an artificial intelligence (AI) text prediction model. More specifically, it resulted from a collaboration with AI, using the GPT model in OpenAI's playground.

By the time you read this book, the use of GPT models to generate text likely will have become somewhat commonplace. However, when I set out to write this book, GPT models were not widely available to the public (as they are now). Consequently, the increased availability and use of such models illustrate how quickly technologies can come onto the scene and change the way people think about what is possible in education, learning, work, and life.

Indeed, AI tools mark what might be considered a significant shift in the possible. Much of what was once only "doable" by humans (and impossible by machines) can now be done more quickly, easily, and, arguably, even better by machines. When used judiciously, AI can serve as a digital partner that can help extend our imaginative capacity to generate and think through new possibilities. Such technologies can also be thought of as "possibility thinking partners" for students, helping them explore and test out new ideas.

The use of AI in education can also intensify debates surrounding what should be taught in schools and how it should be taught, given the accessibility of "ready-made" information and the increasing availability of digital tools that can produce meaningful products and artifacts based on that information. Of course, as with any innovation, AI can be misused and has its limits.

Consequently, the use of AI chatbots raises serious questions about what such tools mean for student learning now and into the future: *Should they be used by students on assignments and to assist them in their learning? If so, how? If not, why not?* We should not approach such questions out of fear of the new or with unchecked optimism, but rather from a principled approach.

Although this book is not about new technologies, advances in AI serve as an example of the kinds of rapid change that can move us to consider new possibilities for education from a principled perspective. As will be discussed throughout this book, any new and transformative possibility or innovation should be approached with a blend of hope *and* active consideration of potentially negative outcomes. Indeed, this book stresses the importance of helping students learn how to take a principled approach to their own creative efforts, by being supported in actively considering and monitoring the benefits and potential costs of the creative contributions they develop and share with others.

In sum, this book invites you to think about and, most importantly, start acting on new possibilities for how we might design transformative educational experiences for young people. In some cases, these possibilities will complement existing educational designs. In other cases, these possibilities will replace current designs. This book is therefore not just about generating new ideas but putting those ideas to the test through action.

As such, each chapter is followed by an "Application" section, which provides protocols and examples that can be used to support the development of actionable possibilities for how to design, test out, and refine new approaches aimed at preparing young people to productively navigate current and future uncertainties.

To that end, Chapter 1 opens with an exploration of the question, *What Do We Owe Students?* This question prompts us to actively consider possible futures and the implications for education. Chapter 2 builds on the themes presented in Chapter 1 and discusses educational designs that aim to reduce uncertainty and prepare young people for *likely futures*.

Next, Chapter 3 pushes our thinking forward by introducing a new model of education called, "uncertainty x design" (UxD), which provides an alternative to existing educational designs and is aimed at better preparing young people for *uncertain futures*.

Chapter 4 focuses on the role that uncertainty plays in generating new possibilities for thought and action and how it serves as a starting point for UxD educational experiences. This theme is further developed in Chapter 5, which focuses on the importance of structuring uncertainty for learning.

This leads to Chapters 6 and 7, which focus on how UxD learning experiences can help young people develop their confidence and competence, producing and acting on new possibilities in the face of uncertainty. Finally, Chapter 8 describes how students can learn how to take a principled approach when acting on uncertainty to help ensure that they are making a positive contribution to their own and others' learning and lives. The book closes with a brief "Avanti," highlighting how the possibilities presented in the book serve as a starting point, which can be carried forward by educators, students, researchers, and anyone interested in working toward more promising educational futures.

Acknowledgments

I'd like to give a very special thanks to David Repetto and Rowan Groat of Cambridge University Press for their interest, encouragement, and patience; my dean, Carole Basile, for her inspiration and support in exploring what's possible in education; the generous donors of my Pinnacle West Presidential Chair endowment; and my colleagues and students at ASU who are making the possible happen in education. I'd also like to thank my friends for their support of the possible. And, as always, my love to Jeralynn and Olivia.

PART I

Approaching Uncertain Futures

CHAPTER I

What Do We Owe Students?

> There is no future without education.
> —Attributed to Rosa Parks
>
> Education is the most powerful tool to change the world.
> —Attributed to Nelson Mandela
>
> The purpose of education is to prepare young people for the future.
> —Guy Claxton[1]

What do we owe current and future generations of young people? Although there are many ways to respond to this question, most agree that we owe them an education that prepares them for the future.[2] Education, viewed from this perspective, represents a kind of promissory note to young people and their families: *If students are willing to put in the time, effort, and resources required, then their educational experiences will help equip them to navigate future uncertainties successfully and productively.*

This promissory note reflects a transactional ethos of education (i.e., "If you learn this now, then you will gain something from it in the future"). The transactional ethos of education is not without critique or limitations,[3] several of which will be explored in this chapter. Regardless of the potential benefits and limitations of a transactional educational arrangement, the more general claim remains that a key goal of education is to prepare young people for the future.

With this in mind, we can then ask, "what exactly does it mean to prepare young people for the future?" The aim of this introductory chapter is to address this question and, in turn, use it as a jumping-off point for the remaining chapters of this book.

---

[1] Claxton, "What's the point of school? Rediscovering the heart of education."
[2] Ibid.; Hannon & Peterson, "Thrive: The purpose of schools in a changing world"; McDiarmid & Zhao, "Learning for uncertainty: Teaching students how to thrive in a rapidly evolving world."
[3] Ambrose, "Discovering and dismantling enormous barriers hindering the transition from transactional to transformational giftedness."

What Does It Mean to Educate Young People for the Future?

One way to understand what it means to educate young people for the future is to recognize that education involves developing students' competence in understanding and doing things that they currently are not able to understand or do. In this way, teaching and learning always and already have a future orientation.

Learning is ultimately about change,[4] which involves movement from one's current state of knowing (or unknowing) and doing (or not yet capable of doing) toward a new state of knowing and doing. And teaching is about facilitating the process of learning. Although there have been debates about whether learners always need teachers and formal instruction to learn,[5] few people would deny that teaching can accelerate and enhance the process of developing students' competence.

Competence development alone is not, however, sufficient to prepare young people for future performance and success.[6] Indeed, even if young people can be successful, but do not believe that they are capable of success, then they likely will give up more quickly in the face of difficulty, avoid taking adaptive risks, procrastinate, and even attempt to avoid engaging in new learning activities.[7] Confidence development is therefore also important for future success.

As will be discussed later in this book, confidence in one's abilities serves as the motivational driver for students to engage with tasks, persist in the face of challenges, seek assistance when needed, and know when to pivot away from dead-ends and toward more feasible goals. Confidence has also been found to be a unique predictor of competent performance, persistence, and future aspirations in various academic and performance domains.[8]

We can therefore say that preparing young people for future success involves developing both their confidence and competence. How do students develop competence and confidence? The obvious answer is through experience. And those experiences can be *direct experiences* (learning by doing plus receiving informative feedback) and *indirect or vicarious experiences* (e.g., learning from watching others who clearly demonstrate

---

[4] Alexander et al., "What is learning anyway? A topographical perspective considered."
[5] Ranciere, "The ignorant schoolmaster."
[6] Bandura, *Self-Efficacy: The Exercise of Control*; Bong & Skaalvik, "Academic self-concept and self-efficacy: How different are they really?"
[7] Elliot et al., "Handbook of competence and motivation: Theory and application."   [8] Ibid.

and even explain what they are doing), or some combination of both indirect and direct experience.[9]

A common goal of most educational experiences therefore involves providing students with direct and indirect experiences aimed at helping them to develop their confidence and ability in learning what is taught. This typically takes the form of having students observe teachers explain and demonstrate what is to be learned, and then provide students with guided practice trying out and receiving feedback on their developing understanding and performance. This arrangement is so seemingly obvious that it hardly requires description.

However, if we are to take seriously the question of how to prepare young people for the future, then it throws a bit of a wrench into this seemingly obvious approach because much of the future is unknowable, which raises the paradoxical question: How can we prepare students for what we do not yet know?

John Dewey, the American pragmatist, highlighted this paradox more than a century ago. As Dewey explained, "it is impossible to foretell definitely just what civilization will be twenty years from now. Hence it is impossible to prepare the child for any precise set of conditions."[10] Dewey's comments should give us pause. Given that the future is unknowable, can education really prepare young people for the future? One way to address this question is to expand our understanding of the future.

Not *the* Future, but Multiple Futures

Expanding our view of the future starts with the recognition that there is not one future, but multiple futures. As the future studies scholar Jim Dator has argued, "The future cannot be predicted because the future does not exist."[11] Dator's assertion aligns with the paradox Dewey highlighted, but futurists offer a way out of this paradox. Specifically, the future is not a singular, yet-to-be-experienced state, but rather represents a plural set of possibilities.[12]

Consequently, one way out of this paradox is to recognize that "there is no future but *multiple futures* with varying likelihoods."[13] Equipped with this understanding, we can then view possible futures as ranging from

---

[9] Bandura, *Self-Efficacy: The Exercise of Control.* [10] Dewey, "My pedagogic creed."
[11] Dator, "What futures studies is, and is not."
[12] Glăveanu, *The Possible: A Sociocultural Theory*; Poli, Handbook of anticipation: Theoretical and applied aspects of the use of future in decision making.
[13] Gall et al., "How to visualise futures studies concepts: Revision of the futures cone."

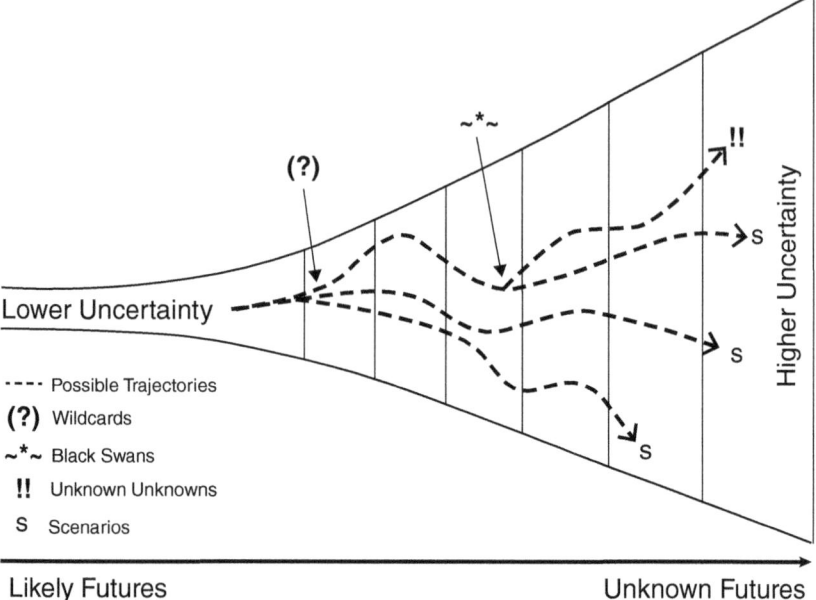

Figure 1.1 Possible trajectories from likely to unknown futures

likely and plausible futures to possible and even seemingly impossible futures. Although impossible futures may be unattainable, it is also important to note that what once seemed impossible can, in fact, become a reality.

When it comes to designing educational experiences aimed at preparing young people for multiple futures, it may therefore be helpful to have a simplified model that represents various trajectories through uncertain futures. Figure 1.1 is an example of such a model.[14]

As illustrated in Figure 1.1, there are various possible trajectories that move from likely futures to unknown futures. No particular future is predetermined. What seems likely now may never come to pass. In fact, even when we find ourselves moving along what seems to be a fixed trajectory, we can experience a "wild card" event, which catches us by surprise and changes our trajectory.[15] Wild cards can occur at the individual level or even at the global level. And considering the possibility of

---

[14] This is a visual representation of varying levels of uncertainty and possible trajectories among likely and possible futures (figure drawn by the author based on ideas and illustrations presented in ibid.).
[15] Ibid.

wild card events, as part of scenario planning, can help us expand our view and push us to consider a fuller range of possibilities and alternatives beyond our current thinking.[16]

COVID-19 serves as an example of a global "wild card" event. Even though global pandemics have occurred in the past (e.g., the 1918 Spanish flu), COVID-19 still caught many people off-guard. Wild card events are considered unlikely possibilities until they occur. And once they do occur, they can have a profound impact on the trajectories and the futures of individuals, entire countries, and global societies.

Black swans are another example of events that can transform possible trajectories through uncertain futures. Like wild cards, black swans are potentially high-impact events that can transform our understanding and experience of unknown futures. Black swan events differ from wild cards because black swans represent seemingly impossible occurrences. They are events that we may be able to imagine but believe that they are not possible. Once we do encounter them, however, they transform our beliefs about what is and is not possible.

As its namesake implies, black swans were once thought to be nonexistent because there was no recorded account of observing them in nature until they were encountered in 1697, on the Swan River in Western Australia, by the Dutch explorer Willem de Vlamingh.[17] Although wild cards and black swans are highly unlikely, they are possible to imagine and anticipate (e.g., there might be another pandemic or there might be extraterrestrial life forms).

In addition to wild cards and black swans, there are "unknown-unknowns,"[18] which we cannot even imagine, but when encountered transform our futures. The iPhone serves as an example. People who lived a century ago likely could not have imagined the Internet, let alone devices such as the iPhone. And when the iPhone was made available, it was difficult to predict the profound impact it would have on the lives of those who have access to it. Although specific unknown-unknowns cannot be imagined or expected prior to their manifestation, they do serve as reminders that even the seemingly unimaginable is a possibility.

Figure 1.1 also illustrates how scenarios can move us beyond likely futures and consider possible and plausible future states. In this way, scenario building can serve as a tool for futures thinking, which can shape

---

[16] Barber et al., "Wildcards: Signals from a future near you."
[17] Hakan, "Philosophy of science and black swan."
[18] Gall et al., "How to visualize futures studies concepts: Revision of the futures cone"; Gustafson, "Strategic horizons: Futures forecasting and the British intelligence community."

our present behaviors and, ultimately, bring about different pathways that can open a broader horizon of possible futures.[19] Indeed, scenarios help us transform the "psychological distance"[20] and abstractness of possible futures by making possibilities conceptually closer, more concrete, and actionable in the here and now.

An extensive example of how scenario building can help us not only imagine but also consider what actions can be taken to bring about new possibilities is presented by the engineer and entrepreneur, Balaji Srinivasan, in his book, *The network state*.[21] According to Srinivasan, it is possible for us to move into what he calls "a network state." A network state reflects a future scenario that describes an organized online community, which is geographically decentralized and connected by the Internet, has a robust digital currency and internal economy, is capable of collective action, and can eventually gain diplomatic recognition and sovereignty from existing and legacy states. Although a network state does not yet exist, Srinivasan describes how movement to such a possibility can be mapped out and, ultimately, realized.

In addition to describing more macro-level futures, scenarios can also help us consider the likelihood of various finer-grain possibilities, including possibilities for new educational designs. Scenarios can thereby help us identify actionable possibilities for how we might move from "what is" to "what might [or should] be"[22] in education. Potential wild card and black swan events can also be considered for each scenario that could change the likelihood and nature of a particular scenario.

In this way, building out different scenarios of future educational designs can serve as a starting point for considering different possibilities (including seemingly impossible scenarios) for the future and how those different possibilities might be realized by acting in the present. More specifically, building scenarios allows us to lift ourselves beyond existing educational designs and map out new possibilities for what education can be. Doing so is not simply an exercise in imaginative thinking but rather enables us to specify actionable steps that we can take to bring about new and previously unimagined possibilities. Scenario building thereby serves as a powerful form of *pragmatic pretense*.[23]

---

[19] Gall et al., "How to visualise futures studies concepts: Revision of the futures cone."
[20] Trope & Liberman, "Construal-level theory of psychological distance."
[21] Srinivasan, "The network state: How to start a new country."
[22] Craft, "Possibility thinking: From what is to what might be."
[23] Beghetto, "A new horizon for possibility thinking: A conceptual case study of Human x AI collaboration."

Pragmatic pretense is a form of possibility thinking that enables us to identify and explore possibilities for transformative action (pragmatic) by deviating from the actual (pretense). Pragmatic pretense blends "what if?" and "as if?" thinking[24] to not only imagine different educational futures (what if?) but also treat them *as if* they are possible. Narrating how each of these possible future educational designs came into being can, in turn, serve as a powerful way of identifying potential pathways into those scenarios.

Ray Kurzweil, the futurist and inventor, for instance, often uses a combination of *what if* and *as if* thinking to imagine, "What if some new invention could be created?" and then describe it "as if" it already exists. Doing so has allowed him and his team to identify actionable steps to realize those new possibilities. He explained this process in a 2022 podcast interview:[25]

> INTERVIEWER: You've invented a lot of things, you've [come up with] and thought through some very interesting ideas. What advice would you give, or can you speak to the process of thinking, of how to think? How to think creatively?
>
> KURZWEIL: ... I think the key issue that I would tell younger people ... is to put yourself in the position that what you're trying to create already exists and then you're explaining...
>
> INTERVIEWER: How it works?
>
> KURZWEIL: Exactly.
>
> INTERVIEWER: That's really interesting. You paint a world that you would like to exist in. As if you think it exists and reverse engineer it ...
>
> KURZWEIL: And then you actually imagine you're giving a speech about how you created this ... well you'd have to then work backwards as to how you would create it in order to make it work.
>
> INTERVIEWER: That's brilliant. And that requires uh some imagination too, some first principles thinking you have to visualize that world ... that's really interesting.
>
> KURZWEIL: And generally, when I talk about things we're trying to invent I would use the present tense as if it already exists. Not just to give myself that confidence, but everybody else who's working on it ... [then you] just have to kind of do all the steps in order to make it actual.

As this snippet from Kurzweil's interview illustrates, using scenarios as a form of pragmatic pretense can enable us to not only imagine something we want to create but also, by treating it as if it already exists, we can then start narrating how it came into being. This, in turn, can bolster our own

---

[24] Craft, "Possibility thinking: From what is to what might be." [25] Lex Fridman Podcast #321.

and others' confidence in figuring out ways to transform the actual by bringing new possibilities into reality.

Finally, Figure 1.1 highlights the fact that uncertainty is ever present in both likely and unknown futures. The figure also illustrates how uncertainty grows as we move from likely futures to unknown futures. Although the increased uncertainty of possible futures can make us feel a bit out of control, a key assertion of this book is that all of us can still be creative agents in our futures.

We can indeed imagine and entertain new and better future possibilities. Doing so can also shape our present actions to increase the likelihood of bringing about those possible futures. The same can be said for young people. Young people are capable of learning how to productively navigate future uncertainties in the here-and-now, but they need opportunities and experience to do so.

This is not to say that experiencing uncertainty is a pleasant experience. Indeed, we often want to avoid or at least reduce uncertainty in our lives, rather than increase it. If, however, we are willing to rethink our relationship with uncertainty and the potential that it holds for bringing about new possibilities now and into the future, then we can be in a better position to recognize that uncertainty serves as an opportunity for creative action.[26] And, as will be discussed in the remainder of this book, supporting students in taking creative action in the face of uncertainty can contribute to their own and others' learning and lives.

Summary and Next Steps

The ideas presented in this book represent scenarios for how educators can design learning experiences that move us from business as usual in education to new and broader possibilities for young people. It thereby serves as an invitation to embrace uncertainty, engage in possibility thinking, and most importantly act on those possibilities. To this end, the protocol and example walk-through presented in Application 1 at the end of this chapter can be used by educators, students, and anyone interested in starting to explore and take action on different scenarios for future educational designs. The protocol can also be adapted and modified to be more tailored and relevant for a particular group and context (e.g., classroom exercise, professional development workshop for educators, community meeting, and so on).

[26] Beghetto, "There is no creativity without uncertainty: Dubito Ergo Creo."

The next two chapters focus on describing two types of educational designs aimed at preparing young people for navigating uncertainty in learning and life. Chapter 2 focuses on the prototypical or default approach aimed at preparing young people for *likely futures*. Chapter 3 then moves us beyond likely futures and invites us to consider how we might design learning experiences aimed at preparing students for the greater uncertainty of *unknown futures*, which is the focus of the remainder of this book.

APPLICATION 1   EXPLORING POSSIBLE EDUCATIONAL FUTURES

Overview

This first application includes a protocol and walk-through aimed at helping educators, students, educational designers, and anyone interested in exploring a range of possible educational futures. Each is briefly previewed and then presented in what follows.

Application 1.1   Educational Futures Protocol

The purpose of this protocol is to engage in a scenario-building exercise with the aim of imagining and describing a range of possible future educational designs to help students learn how to better navigate uncertainty in their learning and lives. To this end, the protocol starts with identifying actionable possibilities for how current educational designs can be transformed into new and more viable alternatives.

Application 1.2   Walk-Through: Educational Futures Protocol

This walk-through is aimed at providing a brief example of how the *Educational Futures Protocol* was used to facilitate a scenario-building exercise exploring a range of possible future educational designs. Although the protocol is best suited for use with a group of two or more people, it can also be used by one person in collaboration with natural language AI chatbots.[27]

This walk-through thereby demonstrates how individual use in collaboration with AI can be generative in providing potentially insightful scenarios. As natural language AI chatbots continue to improve and become increasingly available, they represent a potentially viable option for individuals who want to use this (and other protocols provided in this book) in partnership with AI.

Application 1.1   Educational Futures Protocol

Group size: 1 to 30+

Process

1. Introduction: A facilitator of the activity describes the purpose of the protocol; this can include introducing participants to consider the

---

[27] The author worked with the GPT model available in the OpenAI playground to produce the walkthrough. The resulting "conversation" was lightly edited by the author to increase readability.

question: *What kind of education do we owe students to better prepare them to navigate current and future uncertainties?*

2. Describe an existing educational design: Briefly describe the features of an existing educational design. This can be a higher-level description (e.g., the educational structure, organization, activities, and experiences) or more tailored and specific (e.g., the features of a particular educational program or course).
   - Provide a description of an existing educational design for a given population in a particular time and socio-cultural context.
   - Describe features of the existing design.
   - What are some strengths and limitations of this existing design? What is working and should be maintained? What should be changed and why?
3. Imagine and describe a range of future educational designs: In this step of the process, participants describe different possibilities for educational designs that can better prepare young people to navigate current and future uncertainties. Participants can be invited to consider new designs that build on existing strengths and address limitations of the current design. Participants should be encouraged to imagine and describe designs based on their likelihood of occurring (ranging from likely and plausible to unlikely and even seemingly impossible). When working in groups, each group can work on scenarios that differ by their likelihood of occurring in the future. Each scenario can then be shared and discussed with the whole group.
4. Clarify: In this step, participants can request additional clarification from anyone (or group) who has presented a scenario to get a better sense of what is being proposed. It is okay if there are not too many specifics as requesting clarification can be a shared discussion aimed at further elaborating on the scenarios, particularly unclear aspects, so that participants can gain a better understanding of the features of the scenarios.
5. Select a compelling design for additional exploration: In this step of the process, participants select one (or more) scenario(s) for further exploration. Participants can then be invited to treat this scenario "as if" it already exists and describe how it came into being (i.e., how was the actual, existing design transformed into this design). Participants can also consider potential strengths (i.e., why this design offers a better alternative to the previous, existing design) and limitations (e.g., potential hazards, barriers, and unintended consequences) of this design; what steps can be taken to build on strengths and proactively

address limitations; and how future wild card or black swan events can impact our ability to bring this design into reality.
6. Reflect: Invite participants to reflect on this scenario-building exercise.
   - What did we learn from this process?
   - What, if any, possibilities can be acted on now to make transformations?
   - What are some next steps that can be taken from these insights?
   - What questions and concerns remain?

Application 1.2   Walk-Through: Educational Futures Protocol

Group size: Human participant (Author) and AI partner.

Introduction: Describe an Existing Educational Design

AUTHOR: Here's an example of a common (although not universal) educational design: Students are taught about an academic topic through some combination of lectures, class discussions, and required readings. The students are all taught in the same way and at the same time. The students are then expected to demonstrate in assignments and tests their individual understanding by reproducing what was taught. What do you think is a key strength of this design?

AI PARTNER: The key strength of this design is that it provides structure and consistency in the learning process. It also allows for a lot of feedback and evaluation. Additionally, there is an opportunity for collaboration between peers, allowing them to work together on the same assignments and share ideas with each other.

AUTHOR: I agree that some level of consistency and structure is important in education. I also agree that evaluative feedback and collaboration are also strengths of this design. What are some key weaknesses?

AI PARTNER: Some key weaknesses of this educational design include an overemphasis on rote memorization, a lack of personalization and customized learning plans, and limited opportunities to explore topics in-depth or from multiple perspectives. Additionally, it can be difficult for teachers to ensure that all students fully understand the material being taught, which can lead to lower overall performance levels.

Moving to Alternative Designs

AUTHOR: I also agree with several of the weaknesses you outline, including lack of depth, personalization, and missed learning opportunities. Another weakness I see is a lack of opportunity for students to develop their confidence and competence in navigating uncertainty because the focus is on learning and reproducing "known-knowns" without opportunities for students to tackle more open-ended and ill-defined problems.

Let's now consider a likely future educational design. This possibility represents "business as usual" in education, whereby much of what already occurs will be represented in the foreseeable future. Although there may be surface-level changes that can better prepare young people to navigate current and future uncertainties, the core educational design remains the same. What would it look like?

AI PARTNER: "Likely Future Educational Design": In this educational design, the core structure would remain largely unchanged. However, there may be an increased focus on providing personalized learning plans to suit each individual student's strengths and weaknesses. There could also be more opportunities for students to engage with open-ended projects or explore topics from multiple perspectives rather than being limited to rote memorization of facts. Additionally, technology such as artificial intelligence (AI) can help provide tailored feedback, which helps to foster self-directed growth outside of classroom instruction hours (e.g., supplementing independent study materials with online coursework platforms).

AUTHOR: Okay, let's next consider a *"plausible" future educational design* that includes new and different design possibilities that are less probable, but still believed to be actionable.

AI PARTNER: A plausible future educational design could include more cross-disciplinary studies that focus on the integration of different subjects. For example, this might involve students studying a combination of psychology and economics to better understand stock markets or combining biology with computer science to understand how medical technology can provide solutions to problems in medicine.

Additionally, there may be an increased emphasis on personalized learning methods which use AI-powered recommendation engines to tailor content based on the interests and abilities of each individual learner. Doing so would provide students with greater autonomy in their learning, while still providing guidance when needed by teachers and mentors.

AUTHOR: Now, let's consider an *"unlikely" future educational design* that includes new and different design possibilities that are unlikely and may not be believed to be actionable.

AI PARTNER: An unlikely future educational design could include the implementation of virtual reality (VR) in classrooms where students interact with a simulated environment that is designed to replicate real-world scenarios. This technology can be used for project-based learning which immerses them in an interactive and engaging way, allowing teachers or mentors to guide their decision-making process through feedback loops without having direct control over it. Additionally, there may also be increased focus on community service integration into curriculum so that students better understand how they directly impact society at large rather than only focusing inwardly.

AUTHOR: Finally, let's consider a *"seemingly" impossible future educational design* that includes new and different design possibilities that are viewed as seemingly impossible to act on.

AI PARTNER: A seemingly impossible future educational design could include the implementation of AI-powered tutors which can operate without direct supervision or intervention from teachers. This technology would be able to adjust learning programs for each individual student's strengths and weaknesses as well as provide meaningful feedback tailored exactly toward their personal needs in order to best facilitate growth and understanding. Additionally, this model may also involve digital courses/assignments that are programmed using natural language processing capabilities, allowing students a more conversational way of interacting with course material rather than having to rely heavily on memorization methods alone.

Additional Exploration

AUTHOR: Let's explore the "plausible" future educational design described. Imagine that this design already exists. Can you tell me a brief story of how it came into being? Be sure to discuss how the common, previously existing design was transformed into this new design.

AI PARTNER: This story begins with a group of forward-thinking educators who were determined to transform the way students learn. They recognized that traditional educational models often lacked personalization and did not always provide enough opportunities for critical thinking, collaboration, or meaningful assessment methods, so they set out on an ambitious journey to improve how knowledge is shared in classrooms around the world.
The team began by introducing more cross-disciplinary studies that allowed students to explore multiple subjects within one course while gaining insights from different perspectives than those traditionally taught in separate disciplines alone.
Next, AI-powered tools like recommendation engines and tutors were implemented to identify individual student's learning paths more accurately as well as provide tailored instruction, feedback, and assessment. Combined, these advancements revolutionized the way knowledge was shared in classrooms across the world, leading to a whole new era of education for students everywhere.

Strengths

AUTHOR: What are the strengths of this design?

AI PARTNER: This design has several strengths which include more personalized learning paths tailored for each individual student's needs, increased opportunities for critical thinking, and collaboration through cross-disciplinary studies or project-based activities. Additionally, AI-powered tools can help ensure that students are given meaningful feedback throughout their educational journey as well as relevant assessments depending on their level of understanding instead of relying solely on rote memorization methods.

Limitations

AUTHOR: What are the limitations of this design? Please describe any potential hazards or negative unintended consequences.

AI PARTNER: There are a few potential limitations of this design. Firstly, there is the risk that students could become overly reliant on AI-powered tools and lose out on important socialization opportunities from peers or teachers due to remote learning platforms being used for classes. Additionally, even though personalized learning plans help with targeting weak spots more accurately, they still have their own set of challenges such as providing sufficient support when needed (which may not be feasible in certain cases). Lastly, having too much information available can lead to overload if goals aren't clearly defined, making it difficult for learners to focus their energy properly without feeling overwhelmed by all they have access to learn!

Wild Card and Black Swan Events

AUTHOR: How might future wild card (unexpected) or black swan (seemingly impossible) events impact our ability to bring about this design?

AI PARTNER: Unexpected or seemingly impossible events could have both positive and negative impacts on our ability to bring this design into reality. On the one hand, certain technological advancements may help increase access for students regardless of geography by providing remote learning opportunities in ways that weren't previously possible (such as developing better AI-powered tutors/recommendation engines).
On the other hand, unexpected economic downturns could lead to budget cuts which might limit initiatives meant to enhance online learning experiences, thus hindering progress toward introducing a more personalized type of education system worldwide.

Reflection

AUTHOR: Let's reflect on this dialogue. What did we learn from this process? What, if any, actionable possibilities can be acted on now to make transformations? What are some next steps that can be taken from these insights? What questions and concerns remain?

AI PARTNER: We have learned that there are many possibilities for transforming the way students learn in order to better prepare them for navigating current and future uncertainties. Some of these include introducing more cross-disciplinary studies and utilizing AI-powered tools such as recommendation engines or tutors to provide meaningful feedback tailored toward individual needs.

A number of actionable steps can be taken now, including investing in technology solutions that enable personalized learning and integrating community service projects or virtual simulations within the curriculum. Some questions remain about:

- How effective certain methods will be at ensuring student engagement?
- What motivates learners the most when tackling new concepts or topics?

Finally, it is important for educators and administrators to continue exploring ways in which course materials can integrate more modern tools such as augmented reality (AR) or natural language processing, so that students have access to truly immersive educational experiences tailored toward their needs.

AUTHOR: Thank you. This has been an interesting exploration. The scenario that I've been thinking about is different from what you presented. It is plausible but will require some changes in the way we all typically think about designing learning experiences. It is not heavily dependent on AI, new platforms, or technologies. Rather, the scenario I have been developing focuses on how we can design structured experiences with uncertainty to provide students with opportunities to develop their confidence and competence engaging with and resolving uncertainty now and into their futures. What do you think?

AI PARTNER: I think that this is an intriguing scenario and one which could potentially benefit students greatly in helping them to navigate current uncertainties. Structured experiences with uncertainty can help develop problem-solving, critical thinking skills, as well as encourage creativity when tackling complex challenges, all of which will be invaluable for future successes both personally and professionally.

Additionally, these kinds of activities should allow learners enough space to make mistakes without feeling pressured by traditional assessment methods (which may not properly reflect their individual progress). There needs to be a focus on providing meaningful feedback at the appropriate intervals throughout the experience so that each student feels like they are taking away something valuable from it no matter what outcomes might have occurred. Finally, there also has to be some way for teachers/mentors to ensure that students are able to remain engaged and successfully complete the task at hand without feeling overwhelmed by all of the open possibilities – which could include providing smaller, more achievable goals along with each challenge.

AUTHOR: Thanks for the supportive feedback. Moving toward new possibilities, such as those we have discussed, is what this book is about.

CHAPTER 2

Designing for Likely Futures

> If you do not change direction, you may end up where you are heading.
> —Attributed to Lao Tzu

> [A river's basic shape] ... is fractal, its structure echoing itself on all scales, from river to stream to brook to creek to rivulet, branches too small to name and too many to count.
> —James Gleick[1]

Schools represent something of a paradox. They provide learning experiences that operate in the "here and now" and are based largely on the certainties of the known past; however, they are focused on preparing young people for engaging with the uncertainties of "not (yet) here" futures.[2] In this way, they reflect how we all seem to approach life. Indeed, although we all live in the present, which is informed by our past, we tend to spend far more time thinking about our futures than our past.[3]

Given that the primary goal of schooling is to prepare young people for unknown futures, it is important to consider the prototypical way in which schools attempt to achieve this goal, including the strengths and limitations of this approach. We can then have a better understanding of how and why we must design and enact new possibilities for educating young people to better equip them for navigating uncertain futures.

At first blush, this may seem like a difficult endeavor because there are many kinds of schools. And what students experience within and across those different kinds of schools is undoubtedly, if not infinitely, complex. When we take a closer look, however, we can see that what appears to be different on the surface is largely based on a similar, repeating pattern.

---

[1] Gleick, "Nature's chaos." [2] Glăveanu, *The Possible: A Sociocultural Theory.*
[3] Baumeister et al., "Pragmatic prospection: How and why people think about the future."

Much like the complex and seemingly different shape of a river, the typical design of learning experiences across and within different schools is like a fractal. It is a "structure echoing itself on all scales,"[4] from school to school, grade level to grade level, class to class, lesson to lesson, and learning activities too numerous to count. Students can and, of course, do experience that similar design in different ways. But the point here is that the basic educational design is largely the same across schools, grade levels, and learning activities. My daughter perhaps described this phenomenon best. At the end of 3rd grade, she wanted to try a "different kind" of school.

During the summer break, we found a school that, by all accounts, appeared to be radically different. After attending that school for less than a month, Olivia told us, "I have something to tell you. I thought this place would be different ... but it's still school." She quickly recognized the similar, deep structure in what was otherwise a seemingly different kind of school. This insight is not unique to my daughter.

Scholars of education have long recognized that the prototypical design of learning experiences tends to be based on a common grammar or structure, even though the surface features may appear to be quite different.[5] The point here is not to say that this similar deep structure of schooling completely lacks value but rather highlights the importance of understanding the logic behind the prototypical design, including its strengths and limitations.

As will be discussed in this chapter, the prototypical design of learning experiences is based on a logic that requires us to work backward from what we can confidently forecast students will likely need to be able to know and do in the foreseeable future. As will also be discussed, this approach not only has its benefits but also has serious limitations with respect to what educational experiences can and should offer young people in preparation for navigating uncertain futures.

Educating for Likely Futures

If we stop to think about it, the prototypical approach to education has long been aimed at designing for *likely futures*. Given that likely futures are somewhat predictable, educators tend to draw on what is already known now in preparation for what we believe young people likely will need to know in the foreseeable future.

---

[4] Gleick, "Nature's chaos."
[5] Tyack & Tobin, "The grammar of schooling: Why has it been so hard to change?"

This ethos is reflected in the often-used response we provide to students when they ask, "why do I need to learn this?" We say, for instance, "You'll need this information in your later schooling, in your job, or in life." In some cases, we can say this with higher levels of confidence (e.g., "Most jobs require some level of collaboration, so you do need to learn how to work with others").

In other cases, we hedge a bit, for example, "Advanced math and some professions require familiarity with Algebra II, so you don't want to limit your opportunities by not learning it now." In still other cases, teachers might resort to a more humorous appeal, "What you learn today will be important to you later in life … because there's going to be a test on it a week from now."

Humor aside, most people would agree that there are *known-knowns* taught in school that will be of value in the foreseeable future. That said, the certainty of the "someday" appeal of focusing entirely on "known-knowns" falls short when we extend our view beyond the *likely* futures and into *unknown future* (see also Chapter 3). At this point, it is important to understand the strengths and limitations of the prototypical approach and the logic on which that approach is based.

Backward Design: Understanding the Logic of Educating for Likely Futures

As mentioned, the prototypical design of education is aimed at designing educational experiences based on *known-knowns*. Known-knowns, in the context of education, refer to existing knowledge and skills viewed as important for students to learn and be able to do. Examples include knowing how to read, write, compute, and other known skills and academic concepts believed to be necessary for students' success now and into the foreseeable future.

The prototypical educational approach is based on a logic of backward design, also known as *designing with the end in mind* and *understanding by design*.[6] Backward design has its roots in similar principles of "reverse" or "back engineering" found in other fields aimed at attempting to understand and reproduce a product or system, such as engineering, computer science, biology, and related fields. In education, the logic of backward design was popularized by educational evaluator Ralph Tyler (1902–1992), who outlined what has been called the "Tyler principle"

---

[6] Wiggins & McTighe, "Understanding by design."

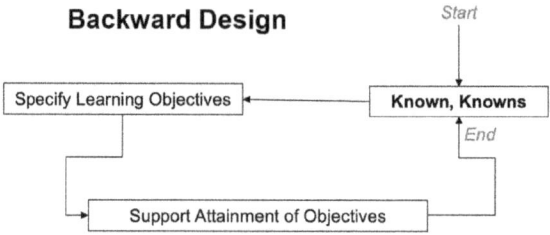

Figure 2.1   Model of backward design

for designing and evaluating curricular experiences in his highly influential 1949 book, *Basic Principles of Curriculum and Instruction*.[7]

The "Tyler principle" represents a rather intuitive process of working backward from a predetermined set of learning objectives. The next step is to design learning experiences to support students' movement toward those objectives and then evaluate whether students have, in fact, attained those objectives. Although educators have long used this backward design approach, Tyler's principle made the logic behind it explicit.

The logic of the backward design approach was further popularized in the late 1990s in the book, *Understanding by Design*, by the educational authors Grant Wiggins and Jay McTighe.[8] The elegant and appealing logic of this approach is represented in the process depicted in Figure 2.1.

As illustrated in Figure 2.1, the process of backward design[9] can be summarized as:

- Specify clear learning objectives and criteria for success,
- Teach students how to efficiently and effectively attain those objectives, and
- Monitor and support students' successful attainment of those learning goals.

Dimensions of Backward Design

Backward design is characterized by lower levels of uncertainty, high levels of structure and support, and a focus on attaining "known-knowns."

---

[7] As of this writing, Tyler's book has been cited over 14,000 times according to Google Scholar.
[8] The first edition of *Understanding by Design* was published in 1998. As of this writing, Wiggins & McTighe's second edition of their book has attained over 13,000 citations in Google Scholar and likely influenced countless scores of educators' approach to curricular and lesson design. Arguably, it is the default mode of curriculum and lesson design in K12 and higher education.
[9] Inspired by the 'Tyler Principle' and Wiggins & McTighe, "Understanding by design."

The use of backward design is most optimal when attempting to prepare young people for likely futures because it helps to limit the universe of possible learning outcomes into a clearly specified set of predetermined goals.

Some level of uncertainty is, of course, ever present in likely futures. However, backward design does (in most cases) effectively mitigate uncertainty by focusing on supporting students in attaining a clearly specified set of learning objectives. Teaching students to learn how to read is an example.

Most people would agree that young people would benefit from developing their reading confidence and competence. And given that there are highly structured, efficient, and generally effective ways of teaching young people how to read,[10] it makes sense that educators would use those highly structured methods to teach students how to read, rather than ask them to learn how to read on their own.

Not all reading programs are successful and, consequently, not all students will benefit from commonly used methods.[11] Some students will need different approaches, technologies, and supports to access and understand written text. Still, the general assertion remains: Reading is one of many skills young people will benefit from in the foreseeable future and backward design can support this goal.

It is therefore not surprising that backward design is the prototypical or *business-as-usual* approach to developing school-based learning experiences for students. Indeed, teachers do and likely will continue to draw on principles of backward design to develop academic lessons, with the hope that what students learn now will be durable enough to support them in doing what seems needed for their futures.

Backward Design Principles and Aspirations
As mentioned, backward design is aimed at minimizing uncertainty by establishing clear learning objectives, teaching students how to arrive at those outcomes, and monitoring whether students have attained those objectives. Teaching based on the logic of backward design is so commonplace that it is even reflected in the pattern of instructional talk between teachers and students. Researchers who have studied instructional talk[12] in

---

[10] Although there is ample research on how to teach reading, approaches to reading instruction have been debated and the research is not always reflected in educational policy and classroom practice (see Castles, Rastle, & Nation, "Ending the reading wars: Reading acquisition from novice to expert"; Snowling & Hulme, "The science of reading: A handbook").

[11] Snowling & Hulme, "The science of reading: A handbook."

[12] Cazden, "Classroom discourse: The language of teaching and learning"; Mehan, "Learning lessons: Social organization in the classroom."

classroom settings have documented a ubiquitous algorithm or rule-based procedure that governs the prototypical form of instructional activity in schools and classrooms.

This procedure called the *Initiate, Respond,* and *Evaluate* (IRE) pattern tightly aligns with the logic of backward design. Specifically, in the prototypical lesson, the first rule in the IRE procedure is for teachers to *initiate* instructional talk by describing or explaining what students are expected to know, and then the teacher poses a *known-answer question* to quickly determine whether students have understood what has been taught.[13]

A known-answer question is a question posed by the teacher that has a predetermined answer. A minimum requirement for the IRE pattern is that the teacher already knows the material, has introduced it to students, and knows the expected answer to the questions posed to students. An example would be: "What is the definition of photosynthesis?"

Once the question is posed, the students are then expected to *respond* to the question with the goal of providing the expected answer (or response) in an expected way. The teacher then *evaluates* the accuracy and adequacy of student responses. If students do not know how to respond or respond inaccurately, then the teacher will provide clarification, the needed corrections, and, in some cases, further instruction.

If students can provide the expected answer in the expected way (or the teacher decides that sufficient time has been devoted to the instructional episode), then the teacher initiates a new IRE episode (e.g., "Now that we know the definition of photosynthesis, can someone provide an example?"). And on it goes. This pattern of talk is so pervasive that it can even be seen in young children playing school (see Figure 2.2)

Figure 2.2 is an image of my daughter (Olivia) playing school. She was in kindergarten at the time and had already become proficient in using the IRE pattern when assuming her imaginary role as "teacher" with her "students" (dolls). She would start out by holding up a picture book and then *initiate* a question about the book, for example, "Jonathan, what did the girl say in this story?" She would then mimic the *response* of one of her students, for instance, [Jonathan] "That she is sad." Next, she would provide rapid, teacher-like *evaluation* and continue on with the pattern, for example, "No, Jonathan, that's not right ... Lucy, what did the girl say?"

At the time, I recall being surprised that Olivia had already learned how to use the IRE pattern in a convincing school-like manner (even though she had not yet spent that much time in school). I then realized, upon a bit

---

[13] Matusov, "Journey into dialogic pedagogy."

Figure 2.2 Olivia playing school

more reflection, that she likely learned this pattern from me as much as from her teachers. I often used an IRE pattern of discourse when reading picture books to her prior to her entering school.

This is not uncommon. In fact, researchers[14] who have studied this pattern of instructional talk report that it is so ubiquitous and "sticky" that parents often use it when attempting to guide the learning of their own children. The stickiness of this pattern of talk, much like many behaviors and beliefs, carries over[15] from parents' and teachers' own prior

---

[14] Cazden, "Classroom discourse: The language of teaching and learning."
[15] Sirotnik, "What you see is what you get: Consistency, persistency, and mediocrity in classrooms."

instructional experiences and is repeated in their future instructional behaviors with their own children and students.

Beyond instructional talk, this same approach, based on the logic of backward design, largely governs most instructional activities in school. Indeed, teachers initiate an instructional task or activity by providing a description of the task and an example of what is to be known. Next, teachers invite students to respond to the task by working alone or with others (e.g., completing worksheets, coming up with examples, and doing homework). Teachers will then evaluate students by inviting them to share their responses in a whole group setting or submit their work for grading.

Strengths and Limitations of Backward Design
The primary strength of backward design is that the approach is already widespread and the logic behind it is easy to explain and compelling: *If* we are confident that students will need to know and be able to do something in the foreseeable future and we already know how to teach it to them, *then* let us focus on teaching that to them (rather than spend time trying to guess what they "might need" to know).

Although this approach has the benefit of reducing educators' uncertainty about what to teach students, it comes with a cost. The primary cost, from the perspective of this book, is that focusing largely (or entirely) on teaching students "known-knowns" unnecessarily limits opportunities for students to learn how to identify their own problems to solve and their own creative ways of solving them.

This is not to say that students will not benefit from what they learn from lessons based on the logic of backward design when navigating unknown futures. Domain knowledge does, of course, play an important role in fortifying imaginative thought and creative action.[16] Indeed, creativity does not occur in a knowledge vacuum.[17] Rather, our creative imagination draws on and extends our existing knowledge and experiences to produce new possibilities for acting on uncertainties we face in learning and life.[18]

The problem with focusing on "known-knowns" arises when we assume that students must first focus on knowledge acquisition in school and then, at some later time, use it to creatively address uncertainties. Indeed, as will be discussed throughout the remainder of this book, when students are supported by more knowledgeable and skilled adults, peers, and even AI, it

---

[16] Baer, "Domain specificity of creativity."   [17] Guilford, "Creativity."
[18] Glăveanu, "Possibility studies: A manifesto"; Vygotsky, "Imagination and creativity in childhood."

is possible for them to creatively draw on relevant knowledge provided by others to tackle uncertainties they face *now* and into the future.

Another potential strength of the backward design approach is that it minimizes uncertainty by providing clear and consistent patterns of instructional behavior, including establishing clear roles and expectations for both the teacher and students. Doing so can reduce confusion and frustration on the part of students and teachers. In the typical backward design lesson, once it is planned, it tends to be somewhat fixed in how it is delivered by teachers and experienced by students.

Teachers do, of course, anticipate and make some adjustments on the fly to help clarify expectations and help support student learning. However, the aim of that support is to help students persist in meeting expectations in expected ways. Consequently, on-the-fly adjustments in the typical lesson are temporary departures from the plan. This can be seen as both a strength and a limitation. The strength is that teachers and students do not get distracted and drift off topic and thereby teachers can maximize students' "time on task."[19]

The drawback, however, is that lessons can become too rigid and thereby result in missed opportunities for more fluid and creative learning possibilities.[20] Indeed, researchers have documented that teachers tend to stick to the lesson-as-planned, even when the lesson-as-lived offers new openings and potentially beneficial departures,[21] such as pursuing an unexpected student idea[22] or changing the instructional process "midstream" when the lesson is not going well.[23]

Although it is understandable that educators would "stick to the plan" instead of risking curricular chaos by "going off-script," this inflexibility can come at the greater cost of supporting deeper learning. As the educational researchers Paul Black and Dylan Wiliam have described:

> [When the] teacher is looking for a particular response and lacks the flexibility or the confidence to deal with the unexpected ... the teacher tries to direct the pupil toward giving the expected answer. In manipulating the dialogue in this way, the teacher seals off any unusual, often thoughtful but unorthodox, attempts by pupils to work out their own answers. Over

---

[19] Godwin et al., "The elusive relationship between time-on-task and learning: Not simply an issue of measurement."
[20] Swayer, "Structure and improvisation in creative teaching."
[21] Aoki, "Spinning inspirited images."
[22] Beghetto, "Nurturing creativity in the micro-moments of the classroom"; Kennedy, "Inside teaching: How classroom life undermines reform."
[23] Clark & Yinger, "Research on teacher thinking."

time the pupils get the message: they are not required to think out their own answers. The object of the exercise is to work out – or guess – what answer the teacher expects to see or hear.[24]

When this pattern takes hold in the way that Black and Wiliam have described, instruction is like a game of intellectual hide-and-seek,[25] whereby students attempt to guess what teachers already know.

Fortunately, not all teachers who use this pattern of talk lack the openness or flexibility to explore students' ideas. In fact, when teachers more judiciously use this approach in conjunction with a willingness to explore the unexpected, it can be an efficient way to quickly check students' understanding while still providing opportunities for students to share and develop their unique and meaningful ideas with others. Teachers who are willing to embrace a bit more uncertainty into their lessons can transform the very nature of the learning experience.

Indeed, rather than quickly evaluating whether a student provides an expected response in an expected way, teachers who are willing to embrace uncertainty can, for instance, briefly explore unexpected ideas and invite other students to do the same. They can then evaluate the potential of those unexpected ideas. Doing so represents a seemingly minor transformation; however, that simple change can result in more generative learning experiences (see Application 2) and is an important first step in moving toward embracing the uncertainty offered by alternative educational designs.

Indeed, exploring encounters with uncertainty first and then evaluating the possibilities resulting from those explorations reflect the core logic of the approach described later in this book. Doing so can result in transformational learning experiences that simultaneously support students' academic learning and their creative potential.[26] Consider, for instance, the results from a multi-method study,[27] which included classroom observations of teacher–student instructional interactions.

Results of those observations indicated that there was a positive association between measures of students' creativity and students' academic achievement when the teacher was willing to use more extended and exploratory patterns of instructional talk. Conversely, a negative relationship between creativity and academic achievement was observed when the

---

[24] Black & Wiliam, "Inside the black box: Raising standards through classroom assessment."
[25] Beghetto, "Ideational code-switching: Walking the talk about supporting student creativity in the classroom."
[26] Beghetto, "Nurturing creativity in the micro-moments of the classroom."
[27] Gajda et al., "Exploring creative learning in the classroom: A multimethod approach."

teacher used a directive and rapidly closing pattern of instructional talk (reflective of the IRE pattern). Finally, no association between measures of student creativity and student academic achievement was observed when the teacher did not explore, develop, or refine students' unexpected ideas.

These findings suggest that embracing uncertainty in an otherwise structured and supportive environment can simultaneously support students' creative expression and academic learning. Conversely, when teachers do not embrace the uncertainty of students' unexpected ideas, then it is likely that there will be no or even a negative relationship between student learning and creative expression. Again, this is not to say that the instruction based on the logic of backward design or even the IRE pattern resulting from that logic should never be used, but rather that it should be used in conjunction with exploration of the unknown because doing so can result in more generative learning opportunities.

Another potential limitation of backward design, however, is that it is often aligned with a transactional approach to learning. As mentioned in Chapter 1, a transactional approach[28] to learning implies that individual efforts will be rewarded in the form of personal gain (e.g., "If you do what is expected and how it is expected in school, then you will likely get better grades, acceptance into college, and better opportunities in work and life"). In this way, transactional learning represents an educational promissory note in which students agree to give time and effort in return for access to knowledge, skills, and training that they expect to be "cashed out" later in life. Such a transactional arrangement, on its own, is not necessarily a weakness if in fact there is later value provided by this type of educational design.

Although people do see (and realize) various forms of value in this transactional arrangement,[29] others do not. Indeed, the almost singular focus on known-knowns can severely constrict the realization of future employment and life possibilities. When this happens, the educational promissory note can start to feel more like a Faustian pedagogical bargain or even Ponzi scheme for students when the promised benefits are not realized in the future.

Consider, for instance, the student loan debt crisis in the United States. As of this writing, the current outstanding balance of student loan debt is

---

[28] Ambrose, "Discovering and dismantling enormous barriers hindering the transition from transactional to transformational giftedness."

[29] National Center for Education Statistics, "Annual Earnings by Educational Attainment." Data reported in May 2022 from the National Center for Education Statistics, for instance, indicate that higher education attainment is associated with higher median earnings (see https://nces.ed.gov/programs/coe/indicator/cba).

$1.78 trillion.[30] Over 43 million Americans have student debt[31] and those who find themselves "overeducated" and "underemployed" or not able to make payments likely view the promissory note of their education as not only bankrupt but also bankrupting them (and society).

Beyond future personal value, another limitation of the transactional approach is that it lacks the expectation for students to contribute to others and the world around them. Indeed, as the psychologist, Robert Sternberg and his colleagues (2022) have argued,

> [Students] do well on statewide or nationwide standardized tests, they earn high grades in school, and perhaps they even attend prestigious universities from which they receive prestigious degrees. *But whether they use their education to benefit anyone beyond themselves is not part of the bargain.*[32]

Of course, educational experiences based on backward design do not inherently reflect a transactional approach or aspiration. Rather, the point is that both tend to run in tandem because backward design and transactional approaches represent the logic and ethos of the prototypical educational experience.

Summary and Next Steps

Focusing on teaching known-knowns, reflected in the logic of backward design, can be thought of as the business-as-usual approach within and across different types of schools. This approach has its share of strengths and weaknesses. It is most beneficial when the goal is to prepare young people for foreseeable futures. However, it has its limits, and when used as the primary approach to education, it unnecessarily restricts the range of opportunities that are available to young people.

Indeed, the central argument of this book is as follows: If we are interested in better equipping students to become active agents in contributing to their own and others' learning and lives, then we need to expand our approach to include experiences that teach them how to engage with and resolve uncertainties they face now and into the future. Put more directly, educating for unknown futures requires different designs and

---

[30] Data based on first quarter 2023 outstanding consumer credit data, reported by the Federal Reserve (www.federalreserve.gov/releases/g19/HIST/cc_hist_memo_levels.html).
[31] Hanson, "Student loan debt statistics."
[32] Sternberg et al., "The Palgrave handbook of transformational giftedness for education," p. v, emphasis added.

the willingness to incorporate those different designs into students' learning experiences.

This does not mean that we abandon educational experiences that are focused on developing students' knowledge and ability to engage with the demands of likely futures. Rather, it requires expanding our designs to include an alternative logic, called Uncertainty x Design (UxD), which is the focus of the next chapter.

APPLICATION 2   MOVING FROM MITIGATING TOWARD EMBRACING UNCERTAINTY

Overview and Preview

This application illustrates how even a brief episode of dialogue can reflect the logic of backward design and the IRE pattern of talk (described in this chapter) and how this approach is often employed to mitigate the uncertainty of unexpected student responses. This application also illustrates how taking an alternative approach to uncertainty can transform the trajectory and outcome of instructional talk – moving from trying to drive students to conform with expected responses and toward more generative learning experiences that embrace, explore, and build upon the uncertainty of an unexpected student response. The application has two parts, which are previewed and then presented in what follows.

Application 2.1 Example and Analysis of the Logic of Backward Design

This application provides an example dialogue between a teacher and a student during a reading lesson, which is based on the logic of backward design. The dialogue is followed by an analysis of the pattern of talk. The analysis includes a discussion of potential benefits and costs of this approach with respect to supporting students in developing both their academic understanding and their understanding of how to productively resolve uncertainty.

Application 2.2 Embracing Uncertainty to Promote Generative Learning

This application presents an alternative approach to the dialogue described and analyzed in Application 2.1. The alternative explores the question, "What if the teacher viewed the uncertainty of student's unexpected responses as opportunities to explore, develop, and extend the student's understanding?" The application also includes a brief analysis and discussion of potential benefits and costs of moving away from the logic of backward design and toward embracing and exploring uncertainty at the micro-level (i.e., in the context of instructional talk).

Application 2.1   Example and Analysis of the Logic of Backward Design

The following is an excerpt from an instructional conversation between a teacher and a student during a reading lesson.[33] There are at least four

---

[33] Adapted from an excerpt of dialogue presented in Skidmore, "From pedagogical dialogue to dialogical pedagogy." In the excerpt provided by Skidmore, other students occasionally chime in.

openings that emerge in the dialogue in which the student provides an unexpected response. The teacher repeatedly uses the IRE pattern of talk, based on the logic of backward design, to force conformity to the expected response. The excerpt is presented below, followed by a brief analysis of the potential benefits and drawbacks of deviating from the "lesson as planned" and toward an alternative direction.

Excerpt

1. TEACHER: Right. So, is it true or false? Docky knew the sound ... erm ... "He heard a dog barking." Did he hear in the first picture on the first page did he hear that barking to be a dog?

2. FIONA: Yes.

3. TEACHER: It wasn't a dog ... Fiona. It was false because it was a fox barking. How does he know it was a fox barking? 'Cause he described it to Mr. Keeping later on and Mr. Keeping said "ha that's a fox bark." Fox ... foxes bark like that. Do you understand? Not really do you?

4. FIONA: Erm. (Fiona *shakes her head*).

5. TEACHER: Why do you think that it's a dog barking? You tell me one piece of information from that story to tell you that it's a dog.

6. FIONA: Because erm foxes don't bark and dogs does ... do.

7. TEACHER: Okay, look at page 6 Fiona. Page 6? Okay. Read it with me.

8. TEACHER AND FIONA: "The next day Rocky saw Mr. Keeping. He told him about the noise."

9. TEACHER: What noise Fiona? What noise?

10. FIONA: The noise what the fox was making.

11. TEACHER: The noise that the fox was making. Which noise was the fox making?

12. FIONA: A dog ... noise. (*Fiona laughs*).

13. TEACHER: He was barking. The fox was barking yeah? So the noise that he heard in the night. So he told him about the noise. Carry on ... reading ... page 6. "That ..."

14. TEACHER AND FIONA: "will be a fox said Mr. Keeping. Foxes bark like that."

However, for the purpose of this application, the adaptation presented only includes the dialogue between the focal student (Fiona) and the Teacher.

15. TEACHER: So. So the noise he heard on that first page was a bark. He thought it might have been a dog.
16. FIONA: It wasn't.
17. TEACHER: But it wasn't a dog. What was it?
18. FIONA: He knew it wasn't a dog.
19. TEACHER: What was it?
20. FIONA: It was a fox.
21. TEACHER: It was a fox. And the statement says on your sheet "He heard a dog barking." Did he hear a dog barking? So is it true or false?
22. FIONA: False.
23. TEACHER: Do you understand?
24. FIONA: Yes.
25. TEACHER: Okay next sentence.

Brief Analysis

As this excerpt illustrates, the entire dialogue is driven by the logic of backward design and reflects the teacher's repeated use of the IRE pattern of discourse. The teacher is operating from known-knowns and has a predetermined outcome in mind. When Fiona is unable to provide that expected outcome, the teacher continues to use the IRE pattern to drive Fiona to that outcome. In some instances (e.g., line 3 and line 13), the teacher even initiates *and* responds in an effort to move Fiona to the expected outcome (e.g., "It wasn't a dog ... Fiona. It was false because it was a fox barking. How does he know it was a fox barking? 'Cause he described it to Mr. Keeping later on and Mr. Keeping said ha that's a fox bark. Fox ... foxes bark like that...").

This pattern is ultimately a "closed" pattern of discourse because any openings provided for the student are quickly closed by the teacher's evaluation of those responses (rather than the teacher opening the pattern by exploring the students' understanding). Figure 2.3 provides a visual depiction that illustrates how openings temporarily emerge whenever the student responds in unexpected ways. It also illustrates how those openings are quickly shut down by the teacher using the IRE pattern until Fiona provides the expected response.

As depicted in Figure 2.3, closed responses dominate this pattern of discourse, representing 84 percent of all the turns of talk (i.e., 21 out of 25

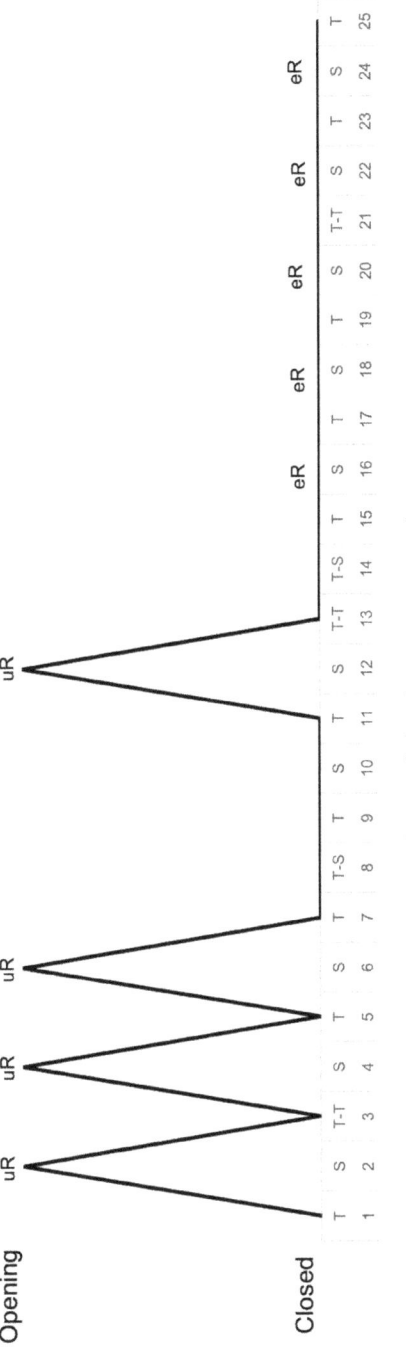

Figure 2.3 Open and closed moments across the interaction

Note. T = teacher; S = student; # = line of dialogue; *uR* = *unexpected response*; *eR* = expected *response.*

turns). There are only four examples of "openings" or unexpected responses (i.e., turns 2, 4, 6, and 12) that eventually get converted to expected responses by turn 16 and those expected responses continue to be reinforced by the teacher across turns 18, 20, 22, and 24.

Potential Benefits

One potential benefit of this approach (at least from the perspective of the teacher) is that it can ultimately fulfill the aim of backward design, which is to get students to respond in expected ways. Another potential benefit is that this pattern of talk mitigates the uncertainty of unexpected responses and does not allow the discourse to drift "off-script" from the planned lesson. In this way, using IRE to "stick to the plan" can allay such concerns that a teacher might have regarding the loss of "time on task." It can also be viewed as a "classroom management" approach, whereby the teacher is attempting to manage what might be perceived as Fiona becoming obstinate and even laughing at her own response by refusing to provide the expected response (e.g., line 12).

Potential Costs

The potential costs of such an approach to students and teachers are twofold. First, even though Fiona does eventually provide the expected response, the teacher cannot know with certainty whether Fiona *actually* understands or believes that foxes bark like dogs. Indeed, she may be simply acquiescing – telling the teacher what the teacher wants to hear – because Fiona may feel that the teacher will persist until Fiona provides the expected response.

The second cost is potentially even more problematic. Indeed, the teacher does not allow Fiona to explain her reasoning. This, in turn, short circuits alternative ways of helping Fiona both understand that foxes can make such noises and even the exploration of broader possibilities for how Fiona might approach and resolve similar moments of "uncertainty" beyond this story.

This teacher might, understandably, assume that such explorations will slow down progress toward attaining other goals of the lesson and "use-up" precious instructional time, and ultimately lead to further confusion for Fiona and other students. However, such assumptions remain untested. Indeed, what if it is possible to do both, even in the same amount of instructional time and "turns" of talk?

The only way to test this possibility is to try it out or consider a counterfactual example. Application 2.2 provides an example of what a more generative alternative that still uses the same amount of time and talking turns (i.e., lines of dialogue) could look like.

Application 2.2   Embracing Uncertainty to Promote Generative Learning

In what follows, an example of an alternative way in which the teacher *could have* responded to Fiona's unexpected responses is provided. The alternative dialogue picks up after the last opening (i.e., unexpected response) in line 12 of Application 2.1, whereby Fiona responded "A dog … noise. (Fiona *laughs*)."

The alternative excerpt[34] presented below provides a counterfactual to what is presented in Application 2.1 and demonstrates one possibility to the question, "What if the teacher viewed the uncertainty of Fiona's unexpected response as an opportunity to explore, develop, and extend Fiona's understanding?"

Alternative Excerpt

…13. TEACHER: Alright Fiona, let's stop for a moment. Why do *you* think Docky thought it might be a dog barking?

14. FIONA: I guess because he didn't know what kind of noise the fox was making.

15. TEACHER: That's right! But imagine you are in that situation – how would you find out if it is a fox or not?

16. FIONA: I would try to look it up or find out about fox noises.

17. TEACHER: Exactly! If you don't know, the best way is to find out more – what other methods could we use?

18. FIONA: We could try to find sounds that foxes make on a computer and listen to them.

19. TEACHER: Good idea! What else?

20. FIONA: I guess we could ask someone who knows a lot about animals – like Mr. Keeping.

21. TEACHER: Very clever indeed!! It sounds like Docky was lucky he had someone around who knew so much about animals – otherwise, this riddle

---

[34] This alternative was written in collaboration with the OpenAI playground GPT model.

wouldn't have been solved at all! Now let's take your ideas one step further – how can we apply this thinking when solving any problem?

22. FIONA: If something we're trying to solve has a lot of stuff that we don't know about, it's probably best to take some time and find out about it before coming up with answers. We need to do our research first.

23. TEACHER: Right on track here too – learning new information can help broaden our perspective which encourages us to think from different angles thus leading toward potential discoveries and inventions! So always remember practice makes perfect. Can you think of an example of how you might use this kind of thinking in your life?

24. FIONA: I could use this kind of thinking when trying to solve a difficult math problem. Instead of just guessing the answer, I can look up different ways to approach it or ask someone who knows more about it for help.

25. TEACHER: Yes, that's a great idea. Okay, Let's move forward with the story now, shall we?

Analysis

In this alternative, the teacher steps away from trying to compel Fiona to provide the expected response and, instead, steps into the uncertainty of Fiona's response. This shift of focus marks an important and alternative "instructional move" by the teacher. Specifically, moving away from trying to get Fiona to understand what the teacher wants to hear and toward the teacher trying to understand Fiona's ideas.

This shift marks an important departure from the logic and approach that the teacher was using and signals a willingness to explore the uncertainty of Fiona's unexpected responses. As a result, the teacher is not only able to help understand Fiona's perspective but also help Fiona understand how the noise could be a fox. Moreover, such a move extends beyond the immediate lesson and goals of the lesson because the teacher sees the unexpected responses as an opportunity to invite Fiona to discuss strategies for how she might resolve similar encounters with uncertainty in other facets of learning and life.

Potential Benefits

There are several potential benefits of taking this alternative approach and embracing the uncertainty of unexpected student responses. One benefit is that it can help the teacher understand what the student is thinking and provide the student with an opportunity to exercise her own agency in figuring out something that is not making sense. Moreover, it represents a both/and approach (discussed in Chapter 3), whereby students can be supported to develop *both* their academic understanding *and* exercise their own creative thinking and ideas. Doing so can not only ensure that students learn the material but also go beyond the material at hand and make a potential contribution to their own and other students' future encounters with uncertainty in learning and life.

Potential Costs
Engaging with the uncertainty of unexpected student ideas does come with some potential costs. One cost is that it can be uncomfortable for the teacher to step into the unknown because teachers may have concerns about drifting away from the plan. Indeed, stepping into the unknown likely will briefly (or even completely) move "off-script" from the planned sequence (as illustrated in lines 13–24 of the alternative script). However, when this happens, teachers can still return to the lesson as planned (as the teacher did in line 25 of the alternative excerpt). Moreover, if it appears that the discussion is getting too far afield, the teacher can also let students know that they will need to return to the "unplanned" ideas and direction later. The key, of course, is that teachers do in fact return to it at some later date (otherwise it can send the message that such diversions are not welcome).

Finally, teachers may be concerned that exploring unexpected ideas will compound student confusion and may even result in behavioral disruptions. Although this is possible, it is also possible that simply driving students to the expected response can also compound confusion, cause behavior disruptions, and even demoralize students, particularly if students do not understand what they are parroting back to the teacher or feel that the teacher is not taking the time to listen to and understand their ideas.

In sum, the potential benefits of exploring the uncertainties of unexpected responses can outweigh the potential costs. The only way to find out is for teachers to trust themselves and their students to explore unexpected openings when they emerge and be open to the generative possibilities that come from embracing uncertainty, even if in small ways.

CHAPTER 3

Designing for Uncertain Futures

> Through questioning the future ... the intention is to move out of the present and create the possibility for new futures.
> —Inayatullah[1]

> Future-making is a collective enterprise. It requires people who imagine, who respond to acts of imagination and who are ready to work together in order to turn imagination into reality.
> —Glaveanu et al.[2]

We all create plans to help focus our efforts and mitigate future uncertainties. Planning, therefore, plays an important role in motivating and guiding our efforts toward the attainment of our future goals. But plans can also impair our performance when they prevent us from being open to more viable alternatives.[3] Moreover, plans that focus on meeting expected outcomes in expected ways can "close the future" rather than "open up" possibilities and, in turn, prevent us from considering and enacting more viable, "alternative futures."[4]

The same can be said for learning experiences based entirely on the logic of backward design. When we habitually overplan student learning by prespecifying all aspects of the learning experience in advance, we attempt to control uncertainty. But doing so comes at the cost of restricting the possibility of more open and generative learning opportunities. And more to the point of this book, we limit opportunities for students to learn how to engage with and productively resolve uncertainty they face now and into their futures.

In such cases, the "tyranny of the lesson plan"[5] severely restricts what teaching and learning can be. Although educating for *likely* futures has its

---

[1] Inayatullah, "Futures studies: theories and methods."
[2] Glaveanu et al., "Dialogical provocations: A creative trialogue."
[3] Masicampo & Baumeister, "Committed but closed-minded: When making a specific plan for a goal hinders success."
[4] Inayatullah, "Futures studies: theories and methods."
[5] Jeffrey Smith, personal communication, August 16, 2008

place, the central argument presented in this chapter (and throughout the remainder of this book) is that preparing young people for uncertain futures requires a fundamentally different logic of design. Prior to describing that logic, it is first important to highlight why a new design logic is needed.

Why We Need a New Design Logic

Much has been made about the importance of infusing twenty-first-century learning skills in school-based learning to better prepare students for the future.[6] What students tend to experience in schools, however, is largely focused on predetermined learning experiences, which are better aligned with likely futures rather than uncertain futures. Indeed, researchers who have explored how often students get opportunities to engage their creative imagination and take creative action in the face of uncertainty have offered somewhat discouraging, albeit not surprising, results.

Guy Claxton, a UK-based researcher, for instance, reported on results from a multi-year survey study of over two thousand 11- to 16-year-old students in the United Kingdom, which asked students to report the most common activities in school. The most frequent response reported by students was "copying from a board or book." Copying was followed by "listen to the teacher talking for a long time" and "take notes while my teacher talks."[7]

The results in the United Kingdom align with results from one of the largest observational studies in the United States (conducted from the 1970s through the early 1980s) of more than 1,000 elementary and secondary classrooms.[8] John Goodlad, the lead researcher on this project, reported that the research team observed about 75 percent of class time was spent on instruction and nearly 70 percent of that time was spent on talking (by telling) from teachers to students. Goodlad went on to report,

> barely 5% of this instruction time was designed to create students' anticipation of needing to respond. Not even 1% required some kind of open response involving reasoning or perhaps an opinion from students.

---

[6] AACTE + Partnership for 21st Century Skills, "21st Century Knowledge and Skills in Educator Preparation"; OECD, "OECD future of education and skills 2030."
[7] Claxton, "What is the point of school? Rediscovering the heart of education."
[8] Goodlad, "A place called school: Prospects for the future."

Yet another example is reflected in a survey item from the Nation's Report Card[9] used to assess how often 8th-grade school students in the United States "learned about or discussed designing or creating something to solve a problem." The results of this survey indicated that the most frequent (45 percent) response for 8th graders, in public schools, was they only "sometimes" had such experiences. Nearly a third (32 percent) indicated that they "rarely" or "never" learned about or discussed creating something to solve a problem and less than a quarter (23 percent) indicated that they "often" had a chance to do so.

A similar pattern was observed in charter and private schools. And this survey only asked whether they "learned about" or "discussed" and not whether they *actually* engaged in these activities. These results underscore the scarcity of actual opportunities students have been given in school for engaging in the imaginative, creative, and innovative work necessary for learning how to navigate uncertainty.[10]

My colleagues and I developed a formative assessment tool to further explore and highlight for educators the opportunities that students are provided in their classrooms to engage with uncertainty and produce imaginative, creative, and innovative products, performances, and services. We explored these opportunities across two studies.

As part of the first study,[11] my colleagues and I examined 268 teacher responses and 5,020 student responses to the Imagination, Creativity, and Innovation (ICI) index, designed to assess opportunities and support for students' ICI work in school. Teachers were asked to report what they viewed would be ideal as well as what they predicted their students would say. Students then rated what they *actually* experienced in their classes.

Although students reported more opportunities than what their teachers predicted for creative and innovative opportunities, students reported significantly less imaginative, creative, and innovative opportunities than what their teachers reported as ideal. These results highlight that teachers recognize, and students report that the number of opportunities for students to engage in such learning experiences is less than ideal.

The second study[12] used a mixed-method (i.e., qualitative and quantitative) approach to examine the kinds of imaginative, creative, and

---

[9] Nations Report Card, "Technology and engineering literacy."
[10] Beghetto, "There is no creativity without uncertainty: Dubito ergo creo."
[11] Renzulli et al., "Development of an instrument to measure opportunities for imagination, creativity, and innovation (ICI) in schools."
[12] Brandon et al., "Examining teachers' perspectives of school-based opportunities and support for student creativity with the ICI Index."

innovative (ICI) work teachers were most proud of and the intended audience of that work. The study also explored whether there were any differences between reports of gifted education teachers and general education teachers as well as any potential grade-level differences.

Results indicate that most teachers provided examples of their own creative teaching practices, rather than student-directed ICI work. And the most common audience for students' ICI work was limited to the school community. No significant differences were found in ICI index scores between gifted education teachers and general education teachers. Elementary teachers (grades 3–5), however, tended to have significantly higher ICI index scores than their middle school colleagues (grades 6–8). These results further highlight that opportunities for these kinds of learning experiences tend to be limited to school-based, teacher creativity projects and tend to diminish as students move from elementary to higher grade levels.

Taken together, the best we can say is that teachers do provide some of these kinds of opportunities some of the time. But many of these opportunities tend to fall short of what teachers would like to provide and what students actually experience. These results further support the need for a new logic for the design of educational learning experiences aimed at preparing students for uncertain futures. More directly, if we are interested in providing students with opportunities that go beyond focusing on known-knowns and are more optimal for unknown futures, then we need to broaden the kinds of experiences we provide to students to engage with and creatively resolve uncertainties they encounter now and into their own futures.

Uncertainty x Design: A New Logic of Educating for Uncertain Futures

Uncertainty x Design (UxD), introduced herein, is a curricular design process that is based on the logic of providing students with opportunities to identify and engage with uncertainties of *known-unknowns* and then support them in imagining and enacting new possibilities for productively resolving those uncertainties.

Known-unknowns refer to ill-defined problems and challenges students and teachers come to *know* through their lived experiences, but do not (yet) know how to address or solve (i.e., *unknowns*). Thereby UxD represents a *forward design* logic, which involves starting with uncertainty and moving forward by producing and testing out possibilities aimed at resolving that uncertainty.

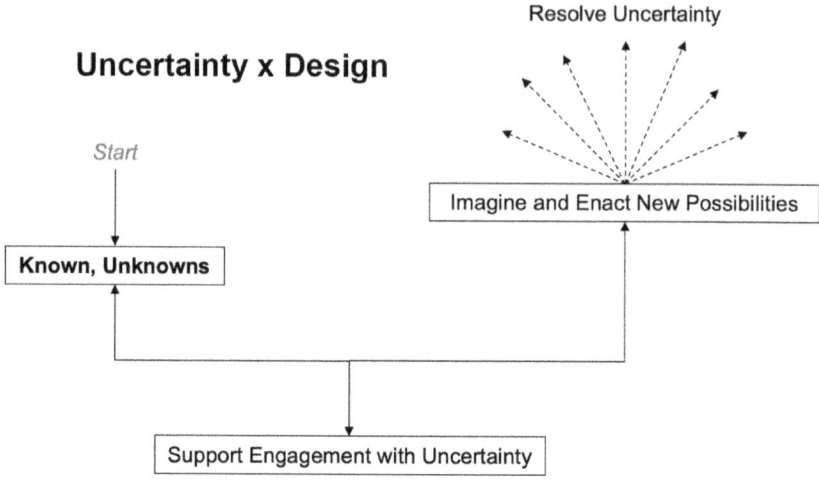

Figure 3.1   Model of the UxD approach

Examples include what can be done for students who experience bullying, social isolation in school, and experience academic stress, anxiety, and other mental health issues. Other examples include everything from the need for positive options and spaces for young people to spend their time during after-school hours to how students might help families who face financial uncertainty in the broader community.

Uncertainty x Design, as its name implies, starts with providing students with opportunities to identify *known-unknowns,* and then move students forward in trying to resolve and address the uncertainty they face. Figure 3.1 provides a visual representation of the logic of the UxD approach.

As illustrated in Figure 3.1, the first step of the process is for students to identify known-unknowns (i.e., ill-defined problems), and then engage the unknown aspects of those problems with the support of teachers and skilled others to imagine and enact new possibilities for addressing those problems.

Dimensions of UxD

The UxD approach significantly increases the level of uncertainty that teachers and students face in teaching and learning (particularly as compared to backward designs) because the UxD learning experiences include more fluid, to-be-determined learning elements. Uncertainty x design

Designing for Uncertain Futures

learning experiences require teachers and students to move from more routine problems and tasks (i.e., known-knowns) toward nonroutine problems and tasks (i.e., known-unknowns).

Again, this is not to say that routine problems lack value or should never be used as part of students' learning, but rather stresses the limits of what such problems and tasks can offer. Indeed, routine problems and tasks represent "pseudo-problems"[13] or "exercise problems"[14] that are more suitable for likely futures because they have ready-made procedures and solutions that can be taught to students.

Conversely, the UxD approach invites students to identify and solve ill-defined problems and tasks[15] that require thinking and acting in new and creative ways. Indeed, as the mathematician, George Pólya, has explained, "The non-routine problem demands some degree of creativity and originality from the student, the routine problem does not,"[16] because non-routine problems have yet to be found, identified, understood, and solved. It is exactly these kinds of problems and experiences that are representative of uncertain futures and thereby the focus of UxD learning experiences.

Uncertainty x Design Principles and Aspirations

The overarching design principle of UxD is structured uncertainty.[17] Structured uncertainty refers to providing students with multiple opportunities to engage with uncertainty in an otherwise structured and supportive environment. As will be discussed in more detail in later chapters of the book, the level of uncertainty and structure can vary in UxD designs, but will still reflect a creative learning experience[18] because they include the subprinciples of:

- Identifying open-ended and nonroutine problems and tasks. UxD designs infuse uncertainty into learning experiences by starting with ill-defined problems and tasks because such problems and tasks invite students to productively engage with uncertainty and generate and enact new possibilities.

---

[13] Getzels, "Creative thinking, problem solving, and instruction."
[14] Robertson, "Problem solving: Perspectives from cognition and neuroscience."
[15] Runco & Chand, "Problem finding, evaluative thinking, and creativity."
[16] Pólya, "On teaching problem solving."
[17] Beghetto, "Structured uncertainty: How creativity thrives under constraints and uncertainty."
[18] Glăveanu & Beghetto, "Creative experience: A non-standard definition of creativity."

- Providing students with opportunities to engage with multiple perspectives. UxD designs also focus on having students share their own perspectives as part of the process of engaging with the perspectives of others. Doing so can help them, test out ideas, challenge assumptions, and generate new possibilities for thought and action.
- Allowing for different and nonlinear approaches. Yet another feature of UxD designs is that they provide the flexibility and support for students to develop and test out different approaches for productively resolving the uncertainty they face in those learning experiences.
- Encouraging students to contribute to others. Finally, UxD designs encourage and expect students to go beyond the self and make a positive contribution to the learning and lives of others.

Taken together, the design principles of the UxD approach orient students toward unknown futures because these kinds of learning experiences help them learn how to produce and enact new possibilities in the face of uncertainty. Importantly, the open-ended nature of the UxD approach does not mean that learning experiences completely lack structure and support. Rather, open endedness is counterbalanced by providing students with high levels of support (e.g., guidance and as-needed assistance from teachers and skilled others inside and outside of the classroom) as well as structured criteria for success (e.g., guidelines regarding timelines and parameters, use of materials and resources, and other relevant academic expectations).

Strengths and Limitations of the UxD Approach

The primary strength of the UxD approach is that it focuses on helping students to learn how to productively navigate uncertainties in the *here and now* so they will be better equipped to shape their own futures. The UxD-based experiences also have the potential secondary benefit of supporting young people in broadening what is possible from learning known-knowns.[19] Indeed, and as will be discussed in the remainder of this book, UxD learning experiences help students transform the actual into new possibilities for thought and action.

Another strength of the UxD approach is that it represents a form of *transformational learning*. Transformational learning provides students

---

[19] Glăveanu, *The Possible: A Sociocultural Theory.*

with opportunities to put their learning to creative use by contributing to their world, even if in small ways.[20] As such, the UxD approach is aligned with what futurists have described as necessary for cultivating *futures consciousness*. Futures consciousness has been defined as:

> the human capacity to understand, anticipate, prepare for and embrace the future. It can be considered as the multiple processes that influence ... how one projects the self and its social surroundings in potential futures, in order to actively adapt oneself to it when it will become the present; and ... how one projects potential futures and adapts their present actions to bring about the ideal future.[21]

A limitation of the UxD approach is that it can be less effective when the goal is to teach students to learn what is already known. Indeed, spending time on UxD learning experiences has, for instance, the potential drawback of taking time away from developing students' speed and efficiency that comes from working through and repeatedly rehearsing routine problems. This is not to say that students will not learn and draw on known-knowns in UxD learning experiences, but rather the focus is not on repetition, memorization, and the reproduction of what is already known.

Another potential challenge of UxD learning experiences is that teachers and students lack familiarity and confidence with such designs. And engaging in such designs can result in experiencing setbacks and failures. Although the UxD approach views setbacks and failures as opportunities for learning and growth, teachers and students may understandably have concerns about these kinds of learning experiences. Consequently, they may be reluctant to try them out.

That said, teachers and students can learn to approach setbacks and failures as an opportunity for learning and growth.[22] And doing so is another facet of the UxD approach (see Chapter 7). Therefore, an important first step when moving toward UxD designs is to take a both/and approach that blends both the use of backward and UxD designs to ensure that teachers and students develop their confidence and willingness to engage with full UxD designs. Indeed, hybrid designs (explored in Application 3 and revisited in Chapter 5) can serve as a helpful transition

---

[20] Sternberg, "Transformational creativity: The link between creativity, wisdom, and the solution of global problems."

[21] Ahvenharju, et al., "Individual futures consciousness: Psychology behind the five-dimensional Futures Consciousness scale."

[22] Manalo & Kapur, "The role of failure in promoting thinking skills and creativity: New findings and insights about how failure can be beneficial for learning."; Beghetto & McBain, "My favorite failure: How setbacks can lead to learning and growth."

in moving from backward designs to designs based on UxD learning experiences.

Finally, another challenge presented by UxD designs is that they require a new way of thinking and acting in the face of uncertainty. And there is no denying the fact that it is challenging to engage with the unknown, rethink how we use time in educational settings, or change our focus from a transactional focus toward a more transformative approach. Just because the UxD approach is challenging, it does not mean, however, that including this approach in students' learning experiences is impossible.

Summary and Next Steps

Helping students to learn how to engage with and resolve uncertainty requires a new logic of educational design. And the UxD approach offers a new logic that can result in many new possibilities for designing educational experiences aimed at supporting this goal. Although this approach, like any educational design, has its strengths and limitations, it does offer a new and promising way of preparing young people for unknown futures. And if we agree that we owe students opportunities to learn how to become active agents in their own futures, then no matter how challenging it may seem, we have a responsibility to try to make it happen. Doing so starts with a willingness to rethink our relationship with uncertainty and view it as an opportunity for transformational learning and not as something that should always be avoided, which is the focus of Chapter 4.

APPLICATION 3 EMBRACING THE UNCERTAINTY OF BLENDED DESIGNS

Overview

This application has two parts. The first part provides a protocol for exploring the uncertainty of blended designs (based on the logic of backward design + UxD). The second part provides a walk-through of the protocol. Both are previewed and then presented in what follows.

Application 3.1 Protocol for Exploring Blended Designs

This first part of the application introduces a protocol aimed at helping educators to consider and explore possibilities for how, when, and why a blended (backward design + UxD) approach might be beneficial for educating young people. It can be used as a thought experiment for individuals or as a tool for engaging groups in the exploratory process.

Application 3.2 Example Walk-Through of the Protocol

This second part of the application provides a walk-through of the protocol presented in Application 3.1.

Application 3.1 Protocol for Exploring Blended Designs

Group size: 1 to 30+

Process

1. Introduction – Familiarize yourself with the basic assumptions and logic of backward design and the UxD approach.
    - Backward design is a curricular design process that starts with specifying learning objectives based on "known-knowns" and then working backward from those objectives to design learning experiences aimed at supporting students in meeting those learning objectives.
    - Uncertainty x design is a curricular design logic that provides opportunities for students to identify and engage with "known-unknowns" and then support them in imagining and enacting new possibilities for productively resolving those uncertainties.

2. Describe the strengths and limitations of each design. Describe as many strengths and limitations as you can for backward and UxD design.
3. Explore possible benefits and use cases for blending backward + UxD designs. In this step of the process, participants describe how the strengths they identified in step 2 can be combined into a blended design, which can be used to address the limitations of each separate design. This step includes providing examples of what the hybrid designs might look like.
4. Clarify and push thinking forward. In this step, participants can request additional clarification from anyone (or group) who has presented a scenario to get a better sense of what is being proposed. Next, participants can work together to push their thinking forward and consider how blended designs might result in transformational learning experiences that can better prepare students for uncertain futures.
5. Reflect – Invite participants to reflect on this scenario-building exercise.
   - What did we learn from this process?
   - What questions remain?
   - What ideas from this process can be developed, tested, refined, and implemented?

Application 3.2   Example Walk-Through of the Protocol

Group Size: Human participant (Author) and AI partner.[23]

Resulting Dialogue

Exploring the Strengths and Limitations of Each Design

AUTHOR: Here are two ways of designing lessons, projects, and activities for students: Backward design starts with identifying learning objectives based on "known-knowns" and supports students in meeting those objectives. UxD is a curricular design that starts with uncertainty and provides opportunities for students to productively resolve those uncertainties. What are some strengths and limitations of each of these designs?

---

[23] The Author structured the GTP-3 interaction by providing a description of forward and backward design (truncated descriptions are reflected above to save space) and then worked through the protocol to explore potential benefits of each design separately and combined. AI responses have been lightly edited for clarity.

AI PARTNER: Backward Design Strengths – Backward design has the benefit of providing a structure for learning activities and objectives. Having these resources available can help to ensure that students have clear expectations, an organized plan to follow, and continued guidance throughout their journey toward mastery.

Backward Design Limitations – Starting with existing knowledge sets limits on how creative or exploratory instruction could be; it is often difficult for learners to come up with unique solutions when starting from known facts.

UxD Strengths – UxD encourages exploration in uncertain terrain where there are no predetermined goals or answers. It allows teachers the opportunity to provide scaffolding as needed while giving their students freedom within this space so they can find novel strategies for problem-solving in open-ended ways.

UxD Limitations – Without having very carefully planned instructions, such experiences can become disorganized, leading to potential loss of focus if not monitored closely by instructors. This could also lead to students feeling lost or frustrated without the direct guidance of a teacher.

Benefits of Blending Designs

AUTHOR: Okay, please describe how combining the strengths of backward and UxD designs can address the limitations of each and result in a stronger hybrid design. Please provide some specific examples of what the hybrid designs might look like.

AI PARTNER: Combining the strengths of these designs can address the limitations of each in a hybrid design. For example, instead of jumping into problem-solving with little to no guidance (forward approach) or starting by presenting tasks based on existing knowledge sets (backward approach), instructors could begin an instruction plan with some exploration and inquiry process.

This would allow learners to become more familiarized with background information about their topic and then find new ways for approaching the topic. This will help ensure that students do not feel completely overwhelmed. Specific examples of this blended approach might include:

- having student research particular STEM topics before conducting lab experiments (e.g., combination of reverse engineering and discovery);
- allowing class discussions regarding current events stories and then challenging them to create persuasive arguments using primary resources; and
- providing small projects at the beginning followed by larger activities that incorporate all previously learned materials.

Integrating backward design and UxD allows instructors greater flexibility when designing curricula while also introducing the element of surprise, which can lead to increased enthusiasm and potentially more meaningful learning experiences.

Clarify and Push Thinking Forward

AUTHOR: Thank you. I agree that there are merits in blending designs. And hybrid designs represent a good, initial step. But I'm interested in going even further toward embracing the uncertainty of UxD, whereby students have an opportunity to identify problems and tasks that matter to them and come up with their own ways of solving them.

I'm also interested in the kinds of designs that push student learning out into the world whereby they can make a transformative contribution to their own and others' learning and lives. I, of course, agree that it is still important to draw on existing knowledge and to help structure the uncertainty that students face. That said, I think we can go much further by developing educational designs aimed at preparing young people for uncertain futures. And, most importantly, students can do much more to make an impact in their world now and into the future. What do you think?

AI PARTNER: I agree there is great potential for educational designs that push further into UxD approaches that allow students to not only draw on existing knowledge but also develop unique solutions within their environment. This type of learning encourages meaningful problem-solving experiences which can help bridge current understanding with new discoveries making a transformative contribution not only in the lives of learners but throughout all communities as well.

One example could be introducing an open-ended project where multiple individuals or groups are challenged to come up with creative ways in which they can informally educate others around them (e.g., peers, family, and community members) about an issue they feel passionate about such as climate change or mental health awareness. Through this kind of approach, we create opportunities for more active participation from all involved, resulting in real-world action taking place beyond just classroom walls!

Reflection

AUTHOR: I agree and think we're on the same page now. UxD experiences that push student learning further beyond the classroom walls are the key aim and aspiration of this book. At this point, let's take a moment to reflect on this process:

- What have you learned from this process?
- What questions remain? and
- What are some insights that can be shared with others about this process?

AI PARTNER: I have learned that combining the strengths of backward design and UxD can create opportunities for learners to become more engaged and motivated in their educational journey while also helping to foster important meta-cognitive abilities. This allows them to find creative solutions which they may not expect while also honing finer skills related to problem-solving within real-world scenarios.

Additionally, I understand how this hybrid approach is an initial step toward creating transformational learning experiences outside of traditional classroom settings where students are capable of making meaningful contributions both now and into the future. Questions that remain include:

- how do we provide adequate guidance throughout these complex projects without becoming overly restrictive or taking away from its open-ended structure? and
- how might educators support collaboration among peers during times when facing uncertainty [and] potential roadblocks (i.e., lack of resources)?

Insights gained from this process could include emphasizing the importance of preparing teachers and instructors ahead of time who will be leading activities like those described. Having them think through all potential scenarios and resources could prove instrumental in helping students to achieve success within these structures.

AUTHOR: I agree. And the following chapters of this book provide insights into your questions and aim to help educators and students realize the potential benefits of embracing the UxD approach.

CHAPTER 4

Start with Uncertainty

> Habit is the deepest law of human nature.
> —Attributed to Thomas Carlyle

> Something new is started which cannot be expected from whatever may have happened before.
> —Hanna Arendt[1]

We tend to be creatures of habit and for good reason. Habits and routines help provide some level of stability and consistency in our lives. That said, most of us like to take occasional breaks from our routines and habits. We want to break free from the "inertia of habit,"[2] otherwise we might feel trapped in a deadening, mechanical existence. We therefore occasionally introduce little ruptures in our habits and routines.[3]

These intentional ruptures often represent somewhat minimal levels of uncertainty, such as trying new foods, watching movies from a genre that we wouldn't otherwise be interested in, and traveling to new locales. These planned disruptions in our routines and habits still cause a mild level of discomfort because they contain some element of risk. We don't know whether we'll like the new food, movie, or locale. But we can take comfort in the fact that we can quickly resolve any unexpected discomfort by no longer eating the new food, turning off the movie, and returning home from our travels.

In this way, planned breaks from our routines represent manageable uncertainties, because they are largely under our control. After all, we decided to introduce them into our lives and we can, in most cases, return to our existing ways of thinking and acting. If we like what we experienced we'll incorporate them into our repertoire of routines and habits – such

---

[1] Arendt, *The Human Condition*.   [2] Dewey, "The psychology of effort."
[3] There are, of course, people who are "thrill seekers" and seek out more extreme, and potentially dangerous, disruptions in what is offered from a more routine existence.

experiences can, in fact, turn into our new favorites (be it a cuisine, movie genre, or vacation spot).

Of course, not all encounters with the unknown are welcomed, planned, or so easily managed and resolved. When we face deeper uncertainties, we need to think and act in new ways to resolve them. When we are successful doing so, we recognize that we can navigate future uncertainties and feel the surge of being the creative authors of our lives.

The Uncertainty x Design (UxD) approach provides opportunities and support for young people to develop their own sense of agency when facing uncertainty in their own learning and lives. When designing UxD experiences for students, it is important to understand that not all forms of uncertainty are the same. Some are more easily resolvable. Others require focused effort and support. And still other forms of uncertainty may never be resolvable.[4] It is therefore important to spend time exploring the nature of uncertainty and the different types of uncertainty students (and we all) encounter in learning and life, which is the focus of the present chapter.

Understanding Uncertainty

As mentioned, we often develop habits and routines to establish a state of experiential stability. In most cases we do not experience the kind of uncertainty that requires us to act and think in new ways. Rather, we are in a state of *indefinite* stability, which represents a generally stable balance among our epistemological beliefs (the nature of knowledge), ontological beliefs (the nature of reality), and existential beliefs (the nature and meaning of our existence). This stability is indefinite, because it can be disrupted at some future point by an encounter with uncertainty.

When we do experience deeper uncertainties we find ourselves moved into a state of unknowing, what the American pragmatist Charles Peirce called a state of "genuine doubt."[5] When we experience this type of doubt, routine ways of thinking and reasoning no longer serve us. What used to work in the past no longer does. And more fundamentally, we may not know how to even think about what we are experiencing.

This type of experience can be deeply unsettling, and we feel a pressing need to resolve the uncertainty we experience as quickly as possible. Indeed, resolving uncertainty has long been viewed by psychological researchers as one of the fundamental motivators (or movers) of human

---

[4] Greene, *Releasing the Imagination: Essays on Education, the Arts, and Social Change.*
[5] Peirce, "Collected papers of Charles Sanders Peirce."

action.[6] When we do encounter uncertainty it can elicit a variety of responses in us, ranging from avoidance, action, or some combination thereof. We therefore find ourselves at a crossroads when we encounter states of unknowing.

Uncertainty can, for instance, elicit an *avoidance* orientation in us and move us away from engaging with the uncertainties we face. This can occur when we believe that there is nothing we can do to resolve a particular unknown in our life (e.g., "I don't spend time worrying about my own mortality, because there's nothing I can do about it."). Avoidance can also occur, because we fear the unknown and worry about potential negative outcomes (e.g., "I have a potentially good and rather unique idea that might help this project out, but I'm afraid people will dismiss it or laugh at me").

The discomfort that uncertainty elicits in us can, at times, be quite profound. And we may understandably want to avoid future uncertainties. Indeed, even though we may have had positive experiences navigating uncertainties in the past, a few bad prior experiences can result in developing an "avoidance orientation" toward future uncertainties, because we tend to overemphasize bad outcomes over good ones.[7] We may therefore come to view uncertainty as something we should generally avoid.

The problem with adopting an avoidance orientation toward uncertainty, rather than learning how to productively engage with it, is that doing so may develop into a sense of worry and inaction. Indeed, prior research has demonstrated that high intolerance for uncertainty tend to view future uncertainties in a negative light, resulting in stress, frustration, and inaction.[8] High intolerance for uncertainty has also been associated with the development and maintenance of worrying, which can decrease confidence and impede effective problem-solving.[9]

Encounters with uncertainty can also elicit in us an *approach* orientation moving us toward action. Approach orientations, in the context of resolving uncertainty, can be thought of as having two forms: *quick resolution* versus *exploration of the possible*. Action for quick resolution is focused on immediately resolving the unpleasant feeling of unknowing that we are experiencing. Although action for resolution has the benefit of quickly

---

[6] Festinger, *A Theory of Cognitive Dissonance*; Kagan, "Motives and development."
[7] Baumeister et al., "Bad is stronger than good."
[8] Buhr & Dugas, "The intolerance of uncertainty scale: Psychometric properties of the English version."
[9] Freeston et al., "Why do people worry?"

eliminating the negative experience of uncertainty, it can come at a cost, which includes a variety of negative cognitive and behavioral outcomes.

Indeed, researchers have described people who feel a greater "need for closure" when facing uncertainty as having the desire to resolve it quickly by finding "an answer on a given topic, *any answer.*"[10] This can severely narrow possibilities and even result in stereotypical, prejudicial, and extremist thinking.[11] Our desire to quickly resolve uncertainty can also curtail our willingness to recognize and act on new possibilities, even when it may be beneficial and necessary to do so.

Mueller and colleagues,[12] for instance, report on two experiments that demonstrated how experiencing uncertainty can interfere with people's ability to recognize the merit of creative ideas, even when such ideas were beneficial for resolving uncertainty. As these researchers explain, this is problematic because it can prevent us from being able to "recognize creativity, perhaps when we need it most."

Conversely, approaching uncertainty as an opportunity for *exploration of the possible* can be beneficial to creative thought and behavior.[13] Indeed, approaching uncertainty as an opportunity for exploration enables us to identify and realize new possibilities for current and future action.[14] Doing so requires adopting a different attitude when it comes to uncertainty. Rather than viewing it as something that is unpleasant and should be quickly resolved or avoided, exploration of the possible requires what John Dewey, the early American philosopher, called an "attitude of suspended conclusion."[15]

This attitude enables us to rethink our relationship with uncertainty by suspending our desire to hastily resolve the discomfort and, instead, slow down to prepare ourselves to inquire into the unknowing. We can then view uncertainty as a starting point for generating new possibilities for thought and action, including an opportunity to exercise our critical thinking by taking time to explore potential benefits and hazards of acting in the face of uncertainty.[16]

Indeed, researchers have documented that people who are willing to suspend conclusion in the face of uncertainty, also known as "tolerance for

---

[10] Kruglanski, "Motivations for judging and knowing: Implications for causal attribution."
[11] Roets et al., "The motivated gatekeeper of our minds: New directions in need for closure theory and research."
[12] Mueller et al., "The bias against creativity: Why people desire but reject creative ideas."
[13] Zenasni et al., "Creativity and tolerance of ambiguity: An empirical study."
[14] Glăveanu & Beghetto, *Pedagogies of the Possible.*   [15] Dewey, *How We Think.*
[16] Beghetto & Anderson, "Positive creativity is principled creativity."

ambiguity," tend to demonstrate higher levels of critical thinking and creativity.[17] In fact, openness to new experiences, which is essentially the willingness to engage with new and uncertain experiences, has consistently been found to be a strong predictor of our ability to generate new thoughts and actions[18] and has also been associated with students' critical thinking skills.[19]

In the context of UxD, providing young people with structured opportunities to experience, engage with, and productively work through uncertainty has the potential to support the development of their confidence and competence in knowing *when* and *how* to engage with uncertainties they face.[20] Indeed, through structured experiences with the unknown, students can learn when it is beneficial to engage with uncertainties (i.e., potential benefits to self and others outweigh the potential hazards) and even when to avoid it (i.e., potential hazards to self and others outweigh the potential benefits). This awareness is a learned behavior that comes through structured and supportive experiences like those offered in UxD designs.

If young people do not have such experiences, then they may fail to see the value in trying to productively resolve the uncertainties they face (e.g., avoiding an opportunity to participate in a community project aimed at addressing a problem in their neighborhood, because their friends are not part of the project).

Conversely, young people may impulsively take unnecessary and potentially dangerous risks in the face of uncertainty, because they have not learned how to reflect on potentially negative outcomes carefully and critically (e.g., a young person taking an unknown pill that someone gave them at a party). In order for young people to learn how to productively respond to uncertainty, they need to have opportunities to view uncertainty as a chance for exploration that, in turn, can help them make informed decisions about whether and how to take action.

Indeed, when young people view uncertainty as a starting point for generating new and potentially transformative possibilities, as is the case in UxD, then they can learn to suspend their impulse to quickly resolve it.

---

[17] Butterscotch, "Exploring the relationship between tolerance of ambiguity and critical thinking"; Zenasni et al., "Creativity and tolerance of ambiguity: An empirical study."
[18] Kaufman, *Creativity 101*.
[19] Clifford et al., "Personality traits and critical thinking skills in college students: Empirical tests of a two-factor theory."
[20] Kaufman & Beghetto, "In praise of Clark Kent: Creative metacognition and the importance of teaching kids when (not) to be creative."

As the early American pragmatist Charles Peirce asserted, "real inquiry begins when genuine doubt begins and ends when this doubt ends."[21] This type of real inquiry is what possibility thinking is all about, because it enables us to produce new possibilities for transforming what *currently is the case* and move us toward *what could and should be the case.*[22]

This is not random guesswork. Rather it is grounded and fortified by prior knowledge and experiences. As mentioned, this doesn't mean that young people need to wait until they have acquired deep levels of academic knowledge prior to generating and enacting new possibilities in the face of uncertainty. Rather, it simply means that they need to be able to access needed information through partnerships with more knowledgeable and skilled others (e.g., outside experts, teachers, more accomplished peers, and so on).

Finally, when students are able to resolve uncertainty, then they are able to return to some sense of stability.[23] Resolving encounters with uncertainty is therefore much like the Zen proverb:

> Before enlightenment – chop wood, carry water.
>
> After enlightenment – chop wood, carry water.

This proverb can be rewritten, so it is applicable for encounters with uncertainty:

> Before encountering uncertainty – experience routine and stability.
>
> After resolving uncertainty – experience routine and stability.

This is not to say that resolving uncertainty does not change us or even the world around us, but rather to highlight that once we resolve uncertainty we often return to a state of *indefinite* stability. Equipped with this understanding of the nature of uncertainty, we can now turn our attention to understanding the different kinds of uncertainty that students and we all face in learning and life.

Not Uncertainty, but *Uncertainties*

Our experiences with uncertainty differ based on how intensely we feel it and how urgently we feel the need to resolve it. One way to think about

---

[21] Peirce, "Collected papers of Charles Sanders Peirce."
[22] Craft, "Possibility thinking: From what is to what might be."
[23] Anderson, *Creativity and the Philosophy of CS Peirce.*

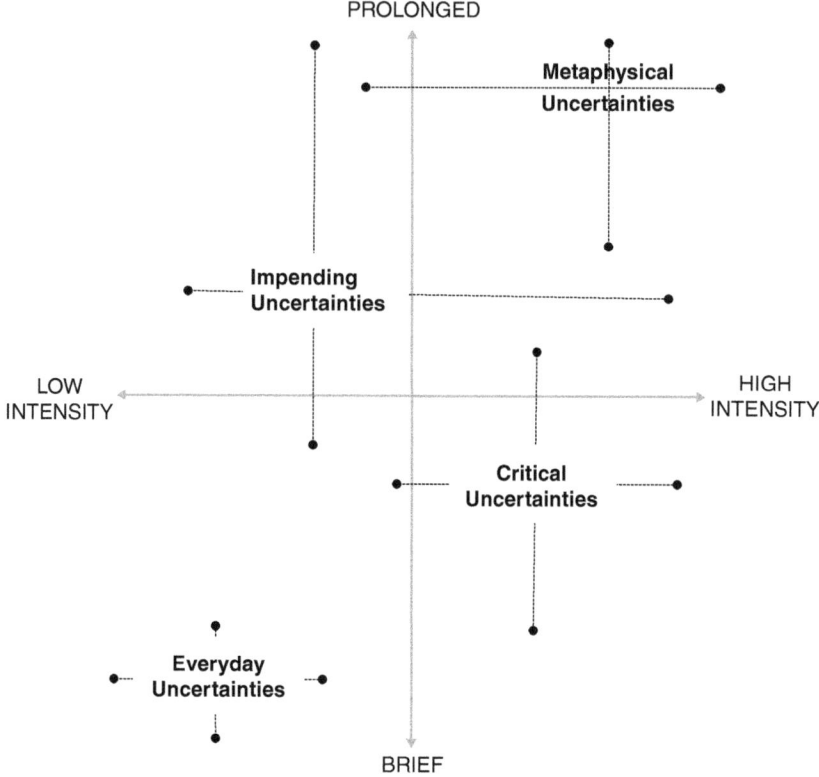

Figure 4.1 Experiences of uncertainty by intensity and duration

different types of uncertainty is to recognize that they differ across at least two different dimensions: *intensity* and *duration*.[24]

Intensity can range from *low* (not occupying much of our thinking and not requiring our immediate attention) to *high* (intruding on our thoughts and requiring our attention). Duration can range from *brief* (temporary or short-lived) to *prolonged* (indefinite or undetermined). Figure 4.1 depicts these different experiences of uncertainty.

As illustrated in Figure 4.1, there are at least four types of uncertainties we can experience: *Everyday Uncertainties*, *Critical Uncertainties*, *Impending Uncertainties*, and *Metaphysical Uncertainties*.

All four types of uncertainties can be incorporated into UxD learning experiences. That said, critical and impending uncertainties represent the

---

[24] Beghetto, "Uncertainty as a lever for change."

most ideal kinds of uncertainties when using the UxD approach, because they are most conducive for prompting students to imagine and enact new possibilities. In the sections that follow, each of these four types of uncertainties will be briefly discussed.

Everyday Uncertainties. They represent brief and relatively low intensity experiences with uncertainty. Examples of everyday uncertainties can include everything from encountering a road closure while commuting to uncertainty about where to take out-of-town visitors for dinner.

Students also experience a broad range of everyday uncertainties in school, including everything from not knowing how their friends will respond to a new outfit, whether an idea during a class discussion will be well received (or rejected), and uncertainty about what questions will be asked in an upcoming history exam.

These kinds of uncertainties are easily resolvable. When we encounter a road closure, the navigation application in our cars or on our phones can easily re-route us. If we are uncertain about where to take our out-of-town visitors for dinner, we can simply ask them what type of food they like, then do a local search for restaurants in the area. Similarly, students will soon find out what their friends think of their new clothes, how their ideas were received during a class discussion, and what questions ended up in their history exam.

As these examples illustrate, everyday uncertainties have a brief temporal window, typically extending from a few minutes to a couple of days. Moreover, they tend to be experienced at a relatively low level of intensity. This is not to say that everyday uncertainties are not distressing, but that they are relatively easy to resolve.

Consequently, everyday uncertainties often do not rise to the level of disruption that requires us to think or act in new ways to resolve them, because they will be resolved with time and routine actions. In fact, if an everyday uncertainty did rise to a higher level of intensity or duration, then it would no longer be an everyday uncertainty and would instead be considered a critical uncertainty.

Critical Uncertainties. These range from moderate to high intensity and typically have a relatively brief duration. Critical uncertainties can include everything from encountering moderately intense unknowns (e.g., presented with an ill-defined problem with a relatively brief timeline) to quite intensely experienced emergency situations (e.g., your car breaks down in a remote area that does not have cell phone service) or a prolonged state of crisis (e.g., worldwide pandemic).

Critical uncertainties require taking new actions in the here and now to resolve them. As with all uncertainties, however, people may choose to defer their action to others, attempt to take action on their own, or work collaboratively with others to resolve the critical uncertainty.

Uncertainty x Design learning experiences can be used to provide students with opportunities to identify and resolve critical uncertainties that they or others face in their learning and lives. Indeed, there are numerous examples of critical uncertainties that young people experience, including some that adults in their lives may not recognize.

An example of a critical uncertainty that many young people face in school is worrying about whether they will continue to be bullied or picked on in school. Although schools have implemented a variety of anti-bullying curricula and prevention measures,[25] the problem persists in sometimes subtler, but still insidious ways. One way that this happens is during lunch time when students feel isolated and rejected by other students.

A teenager from California, named Natalie Hampton, recognized this as a critical uncertainty based on her own experience. Given that she believed this problem had not been sufficiently addressed, she worked to develop a mobile app, called "Sit With Us" that provides a way of finding other students to sit with during lunch time.[26] The app has already had a broad impact with it being downloaded more than 100,000 times in seven countries.[27]

Although young people can identify and address critical uncertainties, they likely will need to collaborate with more experienced and skilled partners, including outside experts, educators, and community members. Indeed, the more uncertain the problem, the more likely it cannot be resolved by just one student or group of students. That said, it is possible that one student or group of students may be able to produce an initial idea that can be developed (with assistance) to solve a complex and critical uncertainty.

Impending Uncertainties. Impending uncertainties refer to moderate or high intensity uncertainties surrounding future or anticipated events. They can operate on a broad timescale from moderate (e.g., weeks, months, and years) to prolonged (e.g., decades and generations). Impending uncertainties are forecasts based on information that is presently at hand and portends complex challenges and unknown futures.

---

[25] Gaffney et al., "What works in anti-bullying programs? Analysis of effective intervention components."
[26] Drake, "Sit with Us creator Natalie Hampton's crusade to help bullied teens feel included."
[27] The Youth Assembly, "Outstanding youth delegate: Natalie Hampton."

Examples of impending uncertainties can include everything from individual concerns about the future (e.g., "How will I manage my retirement and future healthcare needs given I haven't saved enough money?") to more expansive national concerns (e.g., "How will states in the Southwestern US survive increasing water shortages and indefinite drought conditions?") and global unknowns (e.g., "What if increasing geo-political tensions result in nuclear warfare?").

Given that actions taken in the present can go a long way in resolving impending uncertainties, they serve as an ideal focus for UxD learning experiences. Indeed, young people are often aware of, concerned about, and willing to act on a variety of impending uncertainties if they are given the opportunity to do so.

Examples of the kinds of impending uncertainties that young people can start addressing now include everything from the impending closure of a skate park in their community, teenage mental health challenges, and lack of funding for a popular extracurricular program. Other examples include exploring what they can do to help address urban food deserts in their cities, divisiveness and bullying on social media, and the list goes on.

Thomas Aldous, aged fourteen, from Pittsburgh, Pennsylvania, for instance, worked on addressing disaster recovery efforts by coming up with and developing an idea for a robotic hand.[28] His efforts were recognized as innovative and viable in helping to address this impending uncertainty. Aldous is not unique or singular in his ability to identify and resolve impending uncertainties. Indeed, young people are often interested in and motivated to make a positive contribution to others and the world around them. They just need the opportunity and support in identifying and engaging with these kinds of learning experiences. Uncertainty x Designs can provide these kinds of opportunities.

Metaphysical Uncertainties. Finally, there are types of uncertainties that we carry with us throughout life. They serve as an overarching backdrop of doubt, including doubting what we know, doubting the nature of our being, and doubting the viability of our existence. These overarching doubts can be chronic and, in some cases, debilitating. They are the kinds of doubts that reflect metaphysical types of uncertainty (e.g., What can we really know about ourselves or anyone else? Are we living in a simulation? Does my existence matter? Would I be the same person if I was born in a different time? What is the meaning of life?).

---

[28] Society for Science, "14-year-old develops robotic hand to help with disaster recovery; Wins $25,000 top award at the Broadcom MASTERS."

Metaphysical uncertainties represent extraordinary unknowns that we may occasionally entertain or even carry with us throughout life. Metaphysical uncertainties thereby have a rather prolonged or even lifelong duration and can range from moderate to high intensity. Although we cannot fully resolve metaphysical uncertainties, we often construct personally meaningful narratives about them, which can play a role in shaping our beliefs, views, and behaviors.

Metaphysical uncertainties likely will not be entertained in most UxD learning experiences, although they could be. A group of students could, for example, create a documentary film aimed at exploring, curating, and sharing different perspectives on how people grapple with the metaphysical question, "What is the meaning of life?"

When experiencing metaphysical uncertainties, we can still feel a general sense of stability in other aspects of our lives even though we are living under the long shadow of unresolvable and potentially disconcerting unknowns. Although it is true that entertaining metaphysical uncertainties may occasionally interfere with young people's and our own learning and lives, such uncertainties are a feature of the lived experience and can also bring meaning, nuance, or at the very least humility to our other creative engagements.

Teacher-Student Dimensions of Knowing and Unknowing

Finally, it is important to highlight the teacher-student dimensions of knowing and unknowing. These dimensions are particularly relevant when designing UxD learning experiences. Indeed, there are various forms of teacher and student knowing and unknowing that can be drawn on. Figure 4.2 provides a visual overview of these dimensions, which are discussed in what follows.

As depicted in Figure 4.2 there are four categories of teacher-student knowing and unknowing, which include:

- Known to Teacher | Unknown to Students: This dimension refers to things that teachers know that their students do not yet (or may never) know. This form of teacher knowledge includes knowledge about academic topics and skills that students do not yet know until they are taught (or learn it on their own). This also includes hobbies, interests, and skills that teachers may know and are capable of doing (e.g., playing music, being a skilled home cook), but are unknown to students.

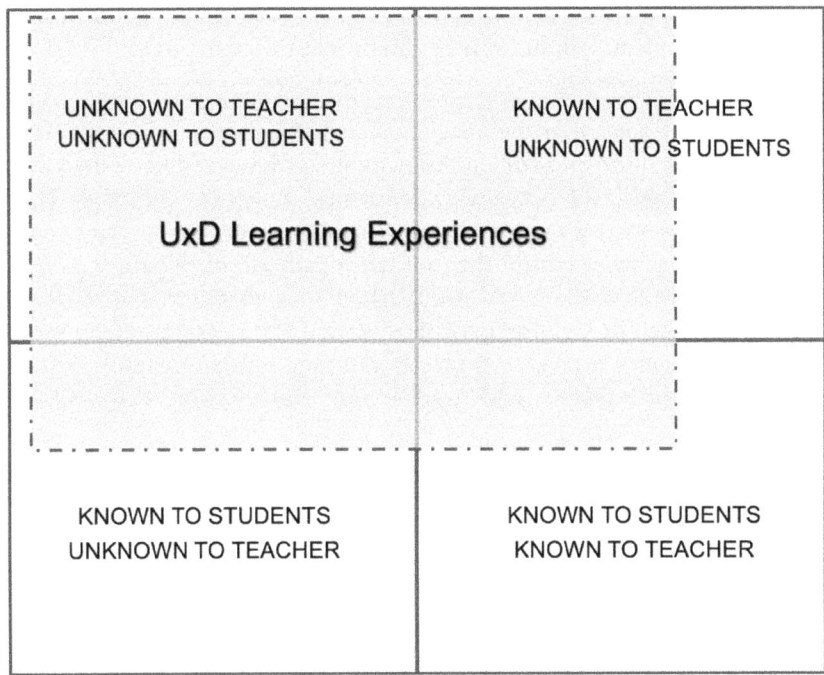

Figure 4.2 Dimensions of teacher-student knowing and unknowing

- Known to Students | Known to Teacher: This dimension reflects teacher-student knowledge, based on shared experiences in school (e.g., academic knowledge, classroom learning activities, and projects) as well as outside of school (e.g., popular knowledge, awareness of current events, and local knowledge).
- Known to Students | Unknown to Teacher: This third dimension represents things that students know and are able to do, but remain unknown to their teachers (and potentially unknown to other peers). This knowledge can include hobbies, interests, information, and skills that students have developed in or outside of school.
- Unknown to Teacher | Unknown to Students: Finally, this fourth dimension represents things that teachers or students do not yet know. Teachers and students may have some familiarity with these unknowns, but lack a full or deep understanding (e.g., "We know that food deserts are a problem in our city, but we don't know the extent or nature of this problem or what we could do about it..."). These can include critical or impending uncertainties that students, teachers, and

other people face. These unknowns can also include problems that are yet to be identified, but can be discovered through UxD learning experiences.

The shaded portion of the image depicted in Figure 4.2 illustrates how *all* dimensions of teacher-student knowns and unknowns can be drawn on when designing UxD projects and learning activities. Although UxD experiences offer the greatest promise when used to explore genuine forms of unknowing reflected in the top-left quadrant of Figure 4.2 (i.e., unknown to both teachers and students), all four quadrants can be drawn on and leveraged in UxD designs. In this way, UxD designs offer a much broader and more expansive form of learning, which can result in new knowledge for students and teachers in and beyond the walls of the classroom.

Summary and Next Steps

Taken together, the various forms of uncertainty described in this chapter, can serve as a basis for designing UxD learning experiences. The goal of these experiences is to assist students in building their confidence and competence. This will aid them in responding to the uncertainties they face now and into their futures. Of course, the "unknowns" that students encounter in UxD designs will need to be combined with supportive structures. This will ensure that students are not overwhelmed. Structuring uncertainty for learning is the focus of the next chapter.

Prior to moving on to the next chapter, it may be helpful to spend some time with Application 4, which is focused on supporting teachers, students, and anyone interested in thinking about the different possibilities for how teacher-student knowns and unknowns can be drawn on and incorporated in UxD learning experiences.

APPLICATION 4 EXPLORING TEACHER-STUDENT KNOWNS AND UNKNOWNS

Overview

This application has two parts. The first is a protocol aimed at exploring different ways teacher and students' knowledge and uncertainties can be leveraged for designing UxD learning experiences. The second part is a walk-through of the protocol, previewed below and presented in what follows.

Application 4.1 Protocol for Exploring Knowns and Unknowns

The purpose of this protocol is to help consider various ways that teacher and student knowing and unknowing can be leveraged for UxD learning experiences.

Application 4.2 Example Walk-Through of the Protocol

The purpose of this walk-through is to illustrate how this protocol can be used to generate new possibilities for UxD designs.

Application 4.1 Protocol for Exploring Knowns and Unknowns

Group Size: 1 to 30+ participants (students, teachers, administrators, community members).

Process

1. Introduction: Start by making sure everyone understands the purpose of the protocol and is familiar with the categories of teacher-student knowing and unknowing summarized below (and described in Chapter 4):
   - Known to Teacher | Unknown to Students: This category refers to a teacher's knowledge (e.g., academic topics, skills, hobbies, and interests), which students do not yet know.
   - Known to Students | Known to Teacher: This shared or compatible form of knowing reflects what students and teachers know from their shared experiences in school as well as outside of school.

- Known to Students | Unknown to Teacher: This third category represents knowledge and skills that students possess (e.g., hobbies, interests, information, and skills developed in or outside of school) but remain unknown to teachers and possibly other peers.
- Unknown to Teacher | Unknown to Students: The fourth category represents things that teachers or students do not yet fully understand or know (e.g., problems they are aware of but do not know how to solve or problems yet to be identified by students and teachers).

2. Describe examples for each of the four categories: Working alone or in groups, identify and describe potential examples of these categories for teachers and students in your school or context. If this protocol is being used by a teacher and group of students, then they can provide actual examples about themselves.
3. Clarify: In this step, participants can request additional clarification from anyone who presented an idea or seek assistance in coming up with examples.
4. How can these categories be used to design UxD learning experiences?: In this step of the process, participants describe different possibilities for drawing on each of the four categories to develop new kinds of learning activities and projects that can support student–teacher collaboration and inquiry into the unknown. Considerations for how these different categories might be combined can also be helpful in generating new possibilities for UxD learning experiences.
5. Share and discuss possibilities: Engage the entire group in a discussion of possibilities and insights for how these various categories can support the design of new types of learning experiences. In this step, clarification can again be requested regarding any possibilities presented or any uncertain aspects of what is being discussed.
6. Reflect: Invite participants to reflect on this application activity.
   - "Let's now reflect on this process. What did we learn from this process? What are some next steps that can be taken from these insights? What questions and concerns remain?"
   - "Imagine three different people had observed our process and discussion. All three people agree that schools can and should prepare students for navigating current and future uncertainties in their learning and lives. One person is very enthusiastic about the ideas we discussed. Another person is not sure about the relevance of the ideas we discussed. And the third person is somewhere in

between the other two. What strengths and limitations would they see in our process and the ideas we generated? What questions and concerns would they ask us to consider?"

Application 4.2   Example Walk-Through of the Protocol

Group Size: Human facilitator (author) and AI partner.[29]

Resulting Dialogue

Known to Teacher | Unknown to Students

AUTHOR: What are some examples of unique and useful things teachers know that can be shared with students, so students are better prepared to navigate current and future uncertainties in their learning and lives?

AI PARTNER: Goal-setting strategies: Teaching students how to create short-, medium-, and long-term goals for themselves can help them stay focused on their studies while also preparing them to manage more complex challenges down the road.
Time management techniques: Many teachers have an arsenal of methods they use to keep their classrooms running smoothly, including time management tips that can be passed onto students, so they know how best to organize and prioritize tasks both inside and outside the classroom.
Problem-solving skills: Learning problem-solving skills is essential for any student navigating challenging situations or topics involving uncertainty or difficulty. Teachers are well equipped with a variety of approaches which could benefit learners seeking out solutions when tackling problems head-on.
Effective communication tactics: Knowing how best to communicate our thoughts, feelings, and ideas as effectively as possible goes beyond simply having good grammar – it's about using language thoughtfully, empathetically understanding different perspectives in conversations around us – this type of knowledge will serve all individuals greatly no matter what life throws at you.
Self-confidence building exercises: Encouraging self-confidence within learning environments isn't always easy but it plays an important role in helping pupils feel prepared when facing whatever lies ahead confidently and without fear getting into the way.

---

[29] The author structured the GTP-3 interaction by providing a description of each of the four categories of teacher-student-knowing-unknowing and then prompts the AI for hypothetical examples of each category (edited and refined by the author). An alternative Human x AI application could involve a teacher adding more specific knowledge to generate more tailored possibilities.

Known to Students | Known to Teachers

AUTHOR: What are some examples of unique and useful things students know and their teachers also know that can be used by teachers to design learning experiences that better prepare students to navigate current and future uncertainties in their learning and lives?

AI PARTNER: Students and teachers understand how collaboration can help in finding successful solutions to complex problems. Developing a classroom culture of open-minded dialogue, brainstorming, trial and error experimentation can build on this knowledge and help students develop the skills they need for problem-solving in uncertain situations.

Teachers and students also understand the importance of creating an environment where students feel safe enough to take risks without fear of judgment – this encourages them to explore new ideas without feeling insecure about making mistakes which further helps prepare them for navigating uncertainties in life outside school.

Finally, students and teachers have some knowledge about how to set goals that are achievable yet challenging so they can be motivated to reach their full potential in learning. This provides a great foundation for designing experiences that encourage students to tackle unfamiliar concepts with enthusiasm, learn how to respond positively when faced with uncertainty or failure, and develop resilience through practice and perseverance.

Known to Students | Unknown to Teachers

AUTHOR: What are some examples of unique and useful things students know that can be shared with teachers so that teachers can design learning experiences that better prepare students to navigate current and future uncertainties?

AI PARTNER: Students often have personal aspirations and interests that can be beneficial for teachers to know when designing projects. Incorporating those aspirations and interests into projects can build enthusiasm and motivation for students to engage with and sustain effort in those projects. Students are also generally well-versed in using digital technologies, this knowledge can be leveraged to help students build key skills like critical thinking, problem-solving, collaboration and creativity in learning experiences that require navigating uncertainty. Many students also have an innate curiosity about their world and a natural desire to explore new things; educators should tap into this enthusiasm by creating meaningful learning opportunities that allow discovery as part of navigating uncertainty.

Unknown to Students | Unknown to Teachers

AUTHOR: What are some examples of things that teachers and students do not yet know (such as problems in their school or surrounding community that

Start with Uncertainty 71

are yet to be identified or addressed) that can be used to design learning experiences that better prepare students to navigate current and future uncertainties?

AI PARTNER: It can be beneficial to explore challenges that students face within their current educational structure – such as a lack of resources or unequal access to quality education – and work on ways for teachers and students alike to improve these issues by devising strategies that could lead toward better distribution of learning materials, more equitable funding for schools, and so on. Also, by looking at different social problems occurring around them (e.g., poverty, homelessness, etc.), educators and students can start to develop a deeper understanding into how they might try to do their part to address such matters.

AUTHOR: Consider all the ideas discussed above. What is an example of how some of the above ideas can be combined to develop UxD learning experience?

AI PARTICIPANT: One way to combine the ideas discussed above is through designing a "Navigating Uncertainties in Learning" course/workshop, where students have an outlet to explore their own ambitions and goals while gaining invaluable knowledge on how to best tackle uncertainties. Another way these ideas can be combined is through a "Community Capabilities" project, where students are encouraged to undertake research surrounding their local community. This can include analyzing problems occurring so they can gain a better understanding of the area and design projects that can be of assistance.

These two activities can empower students to negotiate the challenging moments in their lives and make a positive contribution. By working together on projects such as these, students learn about collaboration and problem-solving within teams and how that can help overcome obstacles. Additionally, they gain an understanding of what issues are present in their local community and sharpen the skills of learning how effective solutions may be reached. The skills learned from participating in either activity will no doubt serve them well when faced with future uncertainties which allows for greater resilience among young adults facing challenges today or tomorrow.

Reflection

AUTHOR: Let's now reflect on this process. What did we learn from this process? What are some next steps that can be taken from these insights? What questions and concerns remain?

AI PARTICIPANT: We learned that there are many unique and useful things both teachers and students know which can be combined to develop learning experiences to better prepare students for navigating current/future uncertainties. We identified two example initiatives that provide opportunities for students to gain invaluable knowledge and understanding taught within the context of their own interests and ambitions.

As next steps, it would be useful to create these activities and give students a sense of ownership over what they learn. Questions remain regarding the best way to involve everyone when designing such projects to ensure engagement.

Imagine Three Different People Observed the Process

AUTHOR: Imagine three different people had observed our process and discussion. All three people agree that schools can and should prepare students for navigating current and future uncertainties in their learning and lives. One person is very enthusiastic about the ideas we discussed. Another person is not sure about the relevance of the ideas we discussed. And the third person is somewhere in between the other two. What strengths and limitations would they see in our process and the ideas we generated? What questions and concerns would they ask us to consider?

AI PARTNER: The enthusiastic person would likely see the strengths in our process by noting that we displayed a great level of collaboration as well as creativity and divergent thinking to come up with solutions. They may also note that the ideas generated could possibly be applied not just on an individual basis but on a school-wide scale, which makes them even more valuable for educators seeking ways to better prepare students for navigating uncertainties.

Limitations they might point out include how these solutions offer only views from two perspectives (students and teachers) when there are other stakeholders involved; it may also be difficult or impossible to implement some of these ideas due to financial constraints or lack of resources/expertise at certain schools.

Questions and concerns: How can results from such activities be best monitored? Will any changes made have long-lasting effects? Which considerations need to be taken when contextualizing existing knowledge within specific learning environments? What different teaching strategies should educators consider using while covering relevant topics? How do marginalized voices fit into this discussion?

AUTHOR: How about the unsure observer?

AI PARTNER: The unsure observer might find strengths in our discussion, such as the diverse ideas we generated and how open and honest communication was considered during problem-solving. However, they may point out that all of these solutions are hypothetical, without any clear view on their success rate or long-term impact.

Questions and concerns: What type of challenges might be identified if community partners were included in this conversation? Could data analytics provide better insight when designing curriculum around certain problems being discussed here? Shouldn't other stakeholders be included to build a more complete picture of the issues at hand?

AUTHOR: How about the in-between observer?

AI PARTNER: The in-between observer may find strength in the process and ideas discussed due to its collaborative approach, as well as combining both students' and teachers' knowledge. They might also appreciate that potential limitations were addressed from a pragmatic standpoint. Other limitations they might point out include lack of information about how to design these projects. Questions and concerns include: How best to measure the success of these methods? What key factors should be taken into consideration while implementing such programs on school grounds? Are there specific implementation issues that need to be addressed to ensure the programs run smoothly?

AUTHOR: Yes, this is just a starting point. More work, thinking, and collaboration is needed whenever we try to design and implement new possibilities for education. The remainder of this book offers additional insights and tools that can move us forward in this effort.

PART II

Designing for Uncertain Futures

CHAPTER 5

Structuring Uncertainty for Learning

> Actively conceiving multiple opposites or antitheses simultaneously . . . plays a role in the development of all types of creativity.
> —Rothenberg[1]

Janus, the mythical Roman god, who simultaneously gazes in opposite directions serves as an analog for recognizing how the blending of opposites is not only possible but can lead to new and emergent outcomes. Emergent outcomes represent something new that results from blending two different things, which are not found in the initial two components that have been combined.[2] A spork, which is a spoon combined with a fork, represents an example of emergent outcome that results from combining two different utensils. A spork shares some properties of both forks and spoons but represents a unique third.

The Uncertainty x Design (UxD) approach can be thought of as a form of Janusian design because it results from combining uncertainty with the structure of design. Indeed, as mentioned in Chapter 3, the primary design principle of the UxD approach is *structured uncertainty.* Structured uncertainty refers to providing students with multiple opportunities to engage with uncertainty in an otherwise structured and supportive environment.

Just like a spork is a unique third that shares some properties with a fork and spoon, the structured uncertainty of UxD experiences is a unique learning experience that shares some features of fully structured backward designs (e.g., predetermined supports, criteria, and guidelines) and the uncertainty people encounter in learning and life (i.e., undefined elements that are not known in advance by teachers or students).

In this way, the structured uncertainty of UxD represents a unique third, because the to-be-determined (TBD) elements of UxD will be decided by students in an otherwise structured and supportive learning

---

[1] Rothenberg, "The Janusian process in scientific creativity, creativity research."
[2] Sawyer, *Explaining Creativity: The Science of Human Innovation.*

environment. The purpose of this chapter is to describe and demonstrate how structuring uncertainty can result in generative UxD learning opportunities aimed at preparing young people for unknown futures.

From Uncertainty to Structure

Whenever we create something new, we move from the uncertainty of the "what could be" toward the structure of "what will be." An artist, for instance, transforms the uncertainty of the blank canvas by adding brush strokes. Each successive brush stroke structures the uncertainty of "what could be" until the final painting is fully realized.

Douglas Anderson, the American philosopher, describes this process in reference to Paul Cézane's famous painting of two card players, "...when Cézane placed a bold brush stroke on a canvas, he began to limit the future of his work."[3] The first brush stroke starts the process of structuring uncertainty and constrains the possibilities for each subsequent brush stroke until the final painting of two card players is realized.

The same can be said for educators who plan lessons and learning activities. Each element of the lesson or learning that teachers define in their planning process, starting with the first one, shapes what that lesson will ultimately become. If teachers define all the elements of the lesson in advance, then they limit the possibilities of what kinds of learning that lesson can support. One way to think about how learning activities are planned or designed is to recognize that most lessons typically have the following four elements:[4]

- The *task* (or problem) – what students are being asked to do;
- The *approach* (or process) – how students are expected to solve the problem or address the task;
- The *outcome* (or product) – what students are expected to produce; and
- The *criteria for success* – the basis for evaluating whether a lesson, activity, or learning experiences has been effective or successful.

The first three elements (i.e., task, approach, outcome) structure the parameters of the learning experience and the fourth element defines the evaluative criteria for determining whether the learning experience was successful, meaningful, or beneficial. In the prototypical approach, such as

---

[3] Anderson, *Creativity and the Philosophy of CS Peirce.*
[4] Beghetto, *What if? Building students' problem-solving through complex challenges.*

Structuring Uncertainty for Learning 79

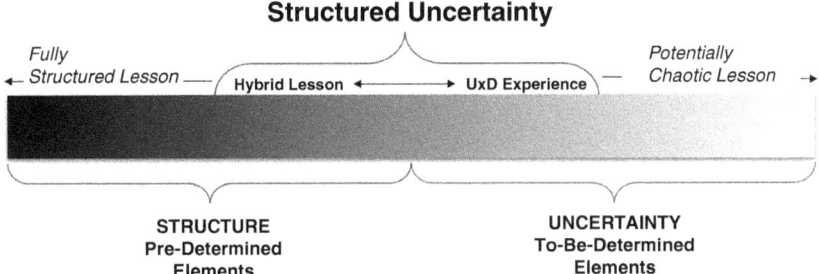

Figure 5.1 Structured uncertainty and the continuum of possible learning experiences

the approach used in backward design, teachers (or curriculum designers) define each of these four elements in advance of teaching.

Once each of the four elements has been defined, then the design process is complete, and the lesson can then be used with students. Viewed from the vantage point of the UxD approach this type of design is overstructured, because uncertainty has been largely removed and the potential for students to generate new possibilities is curtailed. Based on the principle of structured uncertainty, however, teachers can transform overplanned lessons and design entirely new learning experiences by blending predetermined elements of a learning activity with TBD elements (see Figure 5.1).

Figure 5.1 depicts a broad continuum of possible learning experiences that teachers can design. The left-most side of the continuum, for instance, represents the backward design of fully planned lessons, because all the elements have been predetermined. Conversely, the right-most side of the continuum represents potentially chaotic experiences because they have too much uncertainty and do not provide students with enough structure, guidance, and support (e.g., "I don't have anything planned today, so do whatever you want for the next 50 minutes").

Uncertainty x Design falls somewhere in between. Indeed, it is the middle range of the continuum, which represents the blending of the structure of predetermined elements with the uncertainty of TBD elements. It is this middle range that represents two types of UxD learning experiences: starter or *hybrid lessons* and full *UxD learning experiences*. Hybrid designs are represented in the more structured end of the UxD range as illustrated in Figure 5.1.

Hybrid designs have more predetermined elements specified by the teacher and fewer TBD elements. A lesson that invites students to come up with their own way to accurately describe a scientific concept would be an example of a hybrid design with low levels of uncertainty and relatively high level of structure. This is because the task, process, and criteria are fully *predetermined* and only the outcomes (i.e., student-generated examples) are *to-be-determined* by students,

Conversely, UxD projects and activities fall in the more uncertain end of the UxD range depicted in Figure 5.1. Uncertainty x Design projects and activities have fewer predetermined elements established by the teacher and more elements to-be-determined by students. Inviting students to work in small groups to invent something new that solves a problem or addresses an unmet need would be an example of a UxD project, because the problem, process, product, and even some features of the criteria for success are largely unknown in advance.

A more detailed discussion of hybrid and UxD designs will be presented later in the chapter and revisited through examples provided in Application 5. At this point, the key insight to be gleaned is the blending principle of structured uncertainty. Educators who understand this blending principle can use it to transform overplanned lessons into UxD learning experiences.

From Fully Structured Lessons to Structured Uncertainty

The principle of structured uncertainty can be used to transform an overstructured lesson into a hybrid or full UxD learning experience. This process, which has been called *Lesson Unplanning*,[5] requires replacing predetermined elements of an existing lesson or activity with one or more of the elements to-be-determined by students. This is much like how creators across domains generate new and more effective possibilities by cutting away excess structure.

Advances in computer programming and machine learning serve as an example. Andrej Karpathy, who was a founding member of OpenAI and the former director of AI at Tesla, described how cutting away excess structure in programming has moved the field of computer science forward.[6] More specifically, Karpathy described how programmers working on computer-based image classification started out by trying to specify everything in advance – writing highly detailed algorithms to try to get computers to correctly identify something in an image, like a dog.

---

[5] Beghetto, "Lesson unplanning: Toward transforming routine tasks into non-routine problems."
[6] Lex Fridman podcast 333.

Although programmers spent a lot of time and effort trying to specify everything that they thought was needed for this task into their algorithms, it was not an efficient or effective process. Eventually, programmers working in machine learning started to move away from trying to specify everything in advance and toward an approach whereby human programmers only specify the basic architecture and relied on machine learning to "fill-in the blanks." This was a more efficient and effective approach and reflects the concept of lesson unplanning and the principle of structured uncertainty.

Another example is how Picasso produced his famous Bull series. Fernand Mourlot has recounted the process Picasso used when he was working in his Paris workshop. As Fernand explained,[7]

> One day ... he [Picasso] started work on the famous bull. It was a superb, well-rounded bull. I thought to myself that that was that. Picasso however continued on and produced a second state and a third, still well-rounded ...

The second and third bulls in the series were more defined. This is not too remarkable as artists sometimes continue to add definition to their work. What is remarkable, however, is that Picasso continued to work on the bulls. Instead of adding to it, he started cutting away details and features of the bulls. Fernand and the others present that day were surprised and somewhat puzzled by this approach:[8]

> And so it went on. But the bull was no longer the same. It began to get smaller and to lose weight ... Picasso was taking away rather than adding to his composition ... And after each change we pulled a proof. He could see that we were puzzled. He made a joke, he went on working, and then he produced another bull. And each time less and less of the bull remained ...
>
> In the end, the bull's head was like that of an ant ... at the last proof there remained only a few lines ... I still remembered the first bull and I said to myself: What I don't understand is that he has ended up where he really should have started! But he, Picasso, was seeking his own bull. And to achieve his one-line bull he had gone in successive stages through all the other bulls. And when you look at the line you cannot imagine how much work it involved.

Figure 5.2 depicts the progression of the bulls Picasso produced in Fernand's workshop (starting with the first lithograph in the top, left corner and ending with the final lithograph in the bottom right of the

---

[7] Lavin, "Picasso's Bull(s): Art history in reverse."   [8] Ibid.

Figure 5.2 Picasso's Bull series lithographs. The series starts in the top left corner, which represents a well-defined bull. Picasso's final, iconic bull is represented in bottom right of the third row.
(Source: "Pasadena, Norton Simon Museum, Picasso P. The Bull, 1946" by Vahe Martirosyan, licensed under CC BY – SA 2.0)

third row). This also reflects the concept of lesson unplanning and the principle of structured uncertainty.

Taken together these examples suggest how teachers can use lesson unplanning to transform an overstructured lesson into *hybrid* lessons by cutting away predetermined elements and replacing them with elements TBD by students. Although hybrid lessons are still largely driven by teachers, they do provide openings for students to engage with uncertainty in an otherwise structured and supportive learning environment.

Even if the changes to the existing lesson are somewhat modest, the resulting hybrid lesson still represents a legitimate (albeit less fully realized) form of structured uncertainty, because neither the teacher nor the students know in advance how those TBD elements will be resolved. Doing so expands the possibilities for learning as compared to the prototypical approach of teaching.

A common approach when teaching math, for instance, involves the teacher introducing one way of solving a particular type of problem. Then the teacher invites students to practice using that one approach to solve additional problems. A hybrid approach is different. A math teacher using the hybrid approach could, for instance, expand possibilities by teaching students how to use a particular procedure to solve a math problem. The teacher can then introduce uncertainty into this lesson by inviting students to come up with as many ways as they can to solve the problem.[9]

By structuring uncertainty in this way, students have an opportunity to expand their learning beyond the one, teacher-taught approach. If, for instance, the group of students was able to work together to generate a dozen novel and accurate approaches, then a student who was only able to generate one or two different approaches now has access to ten or eleven additional approaches. Even the teacher could learn from this hybrid lesson. If, for example, the teacher initially knew only nine ways to solve the problem that teacher would have the benefit of learning three new, student-generated ways of solving the problem.

Although hybrid lessons can provide valuable learning opportunities, they are just a starting point. Indeed, just like the cantina in the *Star Wars* movie served as the threshold between Luke Skywalker's ordinary existence and fantastical quest that he was about to embark on, hybrid lessons only represent the threshold between prototypical lessons and the more expansive possibilities offered by UxD learning experiences.

From Hybrid to UxD Learning Experiences

Compared to hybrid designs, UxD projects and learning activities are the most transformative representation of structured uncertainty. Although UxD projects have a higher level of uncertainty and the fewest predetermined elements, they are still structured by a supportive learning environment. In this way, UxD projects move students into the driver's seat of designing their learning experiences. Importantly, UxD projects decenter, but do not replace, the teachers' role as designer.

Indeed, teachers still play a critical, supportive role by establishing a structured learning environment to ensure that students are not overwhelmed by assuming the role of project designer. Teachers also play a role in shaping the criteria and parameters of UxD designs. Invention-based projects and contests[10] serve as an example. These kinds of projects involve teachers supporting students in creating something new to address a problem or need across a wide range of domains, including agriculture, animal care, education, fashion, environmental sustainability, safety, and so on.

---

[9] Niu & Zhou, "Creativity in mathematics teaching."
[10] Henry Ford Foundation, "A framework using the steps of the invention process."

Legacy projects[11] serve as another example, which is even more closely aligned with the UxD approach. Legacy projects are based on the four elements of learning activities (i.e., task, approach, outcome, criteria for success), but infuse to-be-determined uncertainty into these elements by posing them as UxD-based questions to students: *What is the problem? Why does it matter? What are we going to do about it?*, and *What lasting contribution will we make?*

Legacy projects aim at supporting students in identifying and addressing a problem that can make a positive and lasting contribution in and beyond their schools and classrooms. Examples include starting a new club focused on caring for others to renovating a broken-down playground in their community.

Regardless of the specific form that a project takes, UxD learning experiences are characterized by four supportive features: *supporting problem finding, supporting students in establishing a rationale for why the project matters, supporting students in taking action to resolve uncertainty*, and *supporting students in making a positive contribution to others*. These features are discussed in the sections that follow.

Supporting UxD Problem Finding

When teachers pose a question, such as "What is a problem or need you want to address?" they support students in moving into the uncertainty of designing their own UxD project. This involves having students identify a problem they want to address or produce something new that does not yet exist. This can be a problem that only students recognize as an issue worth addressing (e.g., "I know my teachers don't realize it, but there is rampant bullying occurring on social media"). It can also be something that they would like to see that has not yet been created or developed (e.g., "I wish we could have a 'study-buddy club' in our school and a space in the school where the club can meet before, during and after school").

The problem can also be an issue that students would like to address in their neighborhood or community (e.g., "We could really help all kids in our community who need new clothing and shoes"). It can even be a problem that impacts their state, nation, and the world (e.g., "We really need to do something to help kids who get bullied on social media").

---

[11] Beghetto, "Legacy projects: Helping young people respond productively to the challenges of a changing world"; Beghetto, *What if? Building students' problem-solving through complex challenges.*

In short, students (not teachers or other adults) are the ones who assume responsibility for identifying and deciding what problem to solve. The problem should be something the students have concerns about and care about addressing. It should be something that matters to them. Consequently, UxD-based problem posing is very different from the routine problems[12] and tasks that students are asked to address in a typical lesson or even hybrid lessons, which tend to be narrowly focused on an academic subject and confined to classroom learning.

Given that students typically have not had the opportunity to identify their own problems to solve or issues to address, they likely will need support engaging in problem finding and problem development. Indeed, students sometimes have a difficult time distinguishing between a problem and a solution, because much of their experience in school has been aimed at addressing problems, but not *finding* problems.

Problem finding,[13] as the name implies, refers to identifying a problem worth solving. When invited to engage in a UxD project, students may, for instance, want to develop an app for a smartphone. Although app development can be the focus of the UxD project, students need to first explain what problem the app solves. With some facilitated discussion and practice, students can learn how to differentiate between a problem (e.g., social isolation in school) and a potential solution (e.g., an app that helps lonely students find companionship in the lunchroom, school activities, and other school events).

Problem finding also involves clarifying and developing a problem.[14] It is easy to underestimate how much time it takes to identify a problem worth solving, because an initial problem may be more complex and nuanced than what students initially thought. Teachers can help students clarify, develop, modify, and even seek out new problems to address. Indeed, sometimes what initially seems to be the problem is not actually the problem, but a feature of a different problem.

Students thereby will need to be supported in generating new possibilities by considering multiple perspectives[15] that can help them further define and clarify the problems that they want to address. This includes supporting them in testing out their assumptions about the problem and being supported in modifying their problems or even seeking out new and different problems (see also Chapter 6). Once students have identified a

---

[12] Pólya, "On teaching problem solving."
[13] Runco & Chand, "Problem finding, evaluative thinking, and creativity."
[14] Brown & Walter, *The Art of Problem Posing.*   [15] Glăveanu, *The Possible: A Sociocultural Theory.*

problem or need that they want to address, the next step is to support them in building a case for why the problem matters.

Supporting UxD Project Rationale

Part of helping students develop and clarify an initial problem or challenge that they have identified is to invite them to build a case for why the problem matters and why it is important to solve it. Because all UxD designs have a goal of benefiting others, students will need to establish the rationale for why addressing this problem will not only benefit them but will also contribute to the well-being of others. This rationale is important for establishing the motivation necessary to engage with and persist when addressing the problem (see Chapter 7).

Developing a rationale is also important for assisting students in finding external partners who can support their work. Indeed, one way of thinking about this rationale is that it serves as a basis for communicating the problem to others who have the expertise, resources, and knowledge necessary to support students in refining and ultimately addressing the problem. Although students are ultimately responsible for establishing the rationale for why the problem matters, teachers still play a key role in facilitating and supporting this process.

Teachers can support the development of the rationale for addressing the problem by orchestrating opportunities for students to learn more about their problem as well as share and receive feedback from others[16] in and beyond the classroom. Addressing the question, "why does the problem matter?" also helps students learn how to resolve uncertainties surrounding the problem by taking into account perspectives from different people, which can help them clarify, modify, and even redefine the problem they want to address.[17] Clarifying the rationale also helps students consider how addressing the problem or issue can make a positive contribution to others.

Again, this is different from what students typically are expected to do in school-based problem-solving exercises, because predetermined problems typically have predetermined rationale (e.g., "You need to learn this because it will be on the upcoming exam"). Supporting students in developing their own rationale ensures that their project is persuasive to them and to other people (i.e., "The reason why we want to design a

---

[16] van Broekhoven et al., "Creative idea forecasting: The effect of task exposure on idea evaluation."
[17] Mumford et al., "Process analytic models of creative capacities."

project that requires building a series of roof-top gardens is because it will benefit people who otherwise cannot afford to buy locally grown produce in our community").

When students are supported in developing an internally and externally persuasive rationale for why it is important to address a problem they have identified, they will be in a better position to act on the problem. This leads to the third support of UxD projects.

Supporting Student Action

Posing questions such as, "Now that you have identified a problem or need worth addressing, how are you going to take action on it?" This question represents a sharp departure from the prototypical prompt that students encounter in school. Although students have some opportunities to learn about ill-defined problems and discuss possibilities for creating solutions to these problems,[18] they rarely get the opportunity to actually solve them.

Providing students with direct experiences to engage with uncertainty and work to resolve it is exactly what the UxD approach offers. These kinds of experiences extend the horizon of possibilities for students because they are aimed at developing students' confidence, willingness, and ability to work with others to tackle uncertainties they face now and into their futures.

As discussed, one reason why students often do not have the opportunity to work toward addressing ill-defined problems and challenges is because they typically have not developed sufficient knowledge, resources, and technical expertise to tackle such problems. Although it is true that students, working on their own, will not likely be able to do this kind of work, it does not follow that students are therefore not ready or capable to solve such problems when working with the support of teachers, peers, and skilled professionals.

Once students can clearly state the problem and the rationale, then they are ready to reach out to skilled others in and beyond their school who can assist them with resources, knowledge, and technical skills necessary to take action and bring their project into reality. Teachers play a key role in supporting students in this effort, including preparing them for the possibility of experiencing setbacks, failures, and successes (see Chapter 7).

---

[18] Nations Report Card, "Technology and engineering literacy."

Regardless of the outcome, teachers can also help students learn from the process, even and especially when their projects do not work out.[19]

Supporting Students' Contribution to Others

Finally, teachers can support students in foregrounding the potential contribution that they can make to others, which is the hallmark of all UxD learning experiences. Consequently, clarifying and monitoring the contribution students are making to others represents a critical design consideration for UxD projects. Teachers play a key role in helping students revisit this aim throughout the entire process of designing, testing out, and implementing their projects. This includes helping students ensure that their work is sustainable.

Again, this is very different from the prototypical learning experience. Typically, once a solution has been attained, the project is over. Even service-learning projects, which operate on a longer timescale, eventually come to an end once the semester or school year ends. Uncertainty x Design projects are different, because the intent is that the work will carry on even after the semester or school year has ended. Teachers can support the sustainable futures of projects by helping students consider how and who will carry the work forward once they move on (see Chapter 8).

The key is to support students in adopting a sustainable and transformative ethos with respect to their efforts. As mentioned in Chapter 3, a transformational ethos[20] focuses on going beyond the self and contributing to others. By foregrounding contributing to others as the aim of UxD projects, teachers can help students make the shift from the prototypical transactional aim of learning experiences and toward the transformative goals of UxD.

Indeed, without initial and constant consideration of the question about contribution, a UxD project could simply be a transactional vehicle for self-gain (maybe even at the expense of others). This is not to say that students cannot or should not personally benefit from UxD designs; indeed they can and likely will benefit both academically and individually from engaging in such work. Rather, UxD projects are guided by the

---

[19] When I served as Director of the University of Connecticut's Innovation House, our motto was, "This may not work, but we will learn from it." This motto helped keep learning in the forefront, even when students' innovative projects did not work out as planned.

[20] Sternberg, "Transformational creativity: The link between creativity, wisdom, and the solution of global problems."

ambitious ethos of trying to make the world a better place for onself and others, even if in small ways.[21]

Finally, teachers can also help support students in knowing when and how to persist, pivot, and even stop and step away from one project idea in pursuit of a more beneficial project, which represents a different ethos compared to what students typically encounter in school. Indeed, the typical message to students stresses the importance of persistence and grit, but not the importance of also knowing when to pursue a different goal. Providing students with the opportunity and freedom to develop their capacity to read a situation and having the confidence in their decision whether to persist or not on a particular effort is an important aspiration of UxD, which is often dissuaded in the prototypical school-based learning experience (e.g., "You can't change topics . . . your team needs to finish the project you started").

Summary and Next Steps

Taken together, UxD learning experiences require a shift in the mindset of teachers, educational designers, and students with respect to how they view the role of uncertainty in teaching and learning. This shift starts with teachers preparing themselves for moving away from *known-knowns* and toward engaging with the structured uncertainty of UxD learning experiences.

Application 5 provides examples and guidelines for designing hybrid and UxD learning experiences. Although examples and strategies can be helpful, the most important takeaway of this chapter and Application 5 is to highlight how the UxD principle of structured uncertainty can teach students to engage with uncertainty and contribute to their own and others' learning and lives, which is the focus of the next chapter.

---

[21] Ibid.

APPLICATION 5 HYBRID LESSONS AND UXD PROJECT EXAMPLES

Overview

Application 5 includes a combination of examples to support the understanding and exploration of the process of *lesson unplanning* and how it can result in *hybrid lessons* described in Chapter 5. This application also includes examples of *UxD projects*.

Application 5.1 Examples of Hybrid Lessons

Application 5.1 provides four examples of *hybrid lessons* and how they were transformed using *lesson unplanning*. The four examples include a middle school science lesson, an elementary school math lesson, a middle school language arts lesson, and a high school science lesson. These examples can serve as a quick way for educators to develop a working understanding of the concept of lesson unplanning and ideas for how existing lessons can be transformed into hybrid lessons. These examples can also be used to support students in participating in the design of hybrid lessons.

Application 5.2 UxD "Starter" Examples

This application provides a series of UxD project examples across elementary, middle, and high school. The "starter" examples have the goal of helping educators and students imagine possibilities and serve as a jumping off point for designing UxD projects.

Application 5.1   Examples of Hybrid Lessons

The following represent examples of fully predetermined lessons[22] that have been transformed into *hybrid* lessons. They represent skeletal or wireframe descriptions of the lesson to illustrate the concept of transforming predetermined lessons into hybrid lessons. The added sentences in the examples below represent predetermined elements that have been replaced by to-be-determined elements.

---

[22] The fully determined lesson examples were generated using GPT3 in the OpenAI playground, by providing a brief description of the four elements of a lesson and requesting GTP3 to generate examples across these different subject areas. The process of designing the elements of a prototypical lesson is so ubiquitous that AI can easily produce viable lesson examples. The TBD elements represent a blend of human and AI generated possibilities.

Middle School Science Example

- *Task:* Students will investigate the properties of water and its environmental impact.
- *Process:* Students will conduct experiments to test the properties of water, such as surface tension, and research the environmental impact of water usage.
- *Product:* Students will develop a presentation on the properties and impact of water.
  - → *TBD Product:* Students will create their own, unique way of demonstrating their understanding of the properties and impact of water.
- *Criteria for Success:* Students will demonstrate a deep understanding of the properties and environmental impacts of water, as well as a high level of creativity in their presentation.

Elementary School Math Example

- *Task:* Students will identify and classify shapes according to their attributes.
- *Process:* Students will use the properties of shapes to identify and classify shapes as either two-dimensional or three-dimensional objects.
  - → *TBD Process:* Students, working together, in teams of two (or three) will decide how to create their own representations of two- and three-dimensional objects (e.g., drawings, clay, paper, digital).
- *Product:* Students will create a poster that identifies and classifies various shapes according to their attributes.
  - → *TBD Product:* Students will arrange their created 2D and 3D objects into a display that they can share with the classroom. How they arrange it is up to them (e.g., a collage, a photo, a physical display).
- *Criteria for Success:* Students will correctly identify and classify all shapes on the poster by correctly categorizing each shape as either two-dimensional or three-dimensional.
  - → *Hybrid Criteria:* Students will correctly classify all the shapes in their display and discuss what they learned from this activity and from the displays of other student teams.

High School Social Studies Example

- *Task:* Students will examine the causes and effects of the French Revolution.

- → *TBD Task:* Students will examine causes and effects of the French Revolution and a change they have experienced in their own life that resulted from similar causes and effects.
- *Process:* Students will research and analyze primary source documents related to the French Revolution to identify key causes and effects.
- *Product:* Students will develop a multimedia presentation on the causes and effects of the French Revolution.
  - → *TBD Product:* Students will develop a multimedia presentation that compares and contrasts causes and effects of the French Revolution with causes and effects that resulted in a change they experienced in their own lives.
- *Criteria for Success:* Students will demonstrate a comprehensive understanding of the causes and effects of the French Revolution, as well as a high level of creativity in their presentation.

Middle School Language Arts Example

- *Task:* Students will analyze a selected literary work.
  - → *TBD Task:* Working in teams, students select a "text" that is meaningful to them (e.g., written literary work, film, digital media) and identify what they believe are the most important themes, symbols, and motifs in the "text."
- *Process:* Students will read and analyze the text to identify key themes, symbols, and motifs.
  - → *TBD Process:* Students in each team will analyze their selected text in collaboration with each other to identify a variety of different themes, symbols, and motifs and decide which ones are most meaningful and important to them.
- *Product:* Students will develop a written analysis of the text and present their findings to the class.
  - → *TBD Product:* Students will present an analysis of the "text" in a creative way (e.g., drama, short video, podcast interview) and share it with others in their class (and potentially beyond their class). After student teams present their analysis, students will engage in a group discussion about how various elements are connected and different across "texts" selected by other student teams.
- *Criteria for Success:* Students will demonstrate a comprehensive understanding of the text and accurately articulate the key themes, symbols, and motifs in their written analysis.

→ *Hybrid Criteria for Success:* Students will demonstrate a comprehensive understanding of the "text" they selected and clearly communicate the key themes, symbols, and motifs that they found most important. Each student will be expected to demonstrate a clear and accurate understanding of theme, symbol, and motif and will provide an individual reflection describing what they learned from the process as well as feedback they received from classmates during their presentations and whole group discussions.

Application 5.2 UxD "Starter" Examples

The following brief narratives[23] serve as UxD project "starter" examples. Educators and students can use these starter examples when first learning about UxD projects to help them imagine their own possibilities for developing UxD learning experiences. The goal is not to implement these hypothetical examples, but to use them as "jumping off points" for students in developing their own UxD projects, which are relevant to their interests and needs they have identified in their school and broader community contexts.

Elementary School UxD Project Example

"*Belonging Matters*"
Imagine a UxD project that was completely designed by a group of 5th grade elementary students to make a positive impact on their school community. The students identified a need to create a more welcoming school environment for students who feel isolated, and they decided to take action. In order to make their school more accepting of all students, they created a student-led club that focused on promoting a sense of belonging for all students.

The students called the club "Belonging Matters" and set out to educate themselves, their peers, and adults on the importance of a more welcoming school environment. The students created a "Buddy System" that

---

[23] Initial examples were generated by the author in collaboration with the GPT3 in the OpenAI playground. The author provided a brief definition of the UxD projects and requested the GTP3 model to generate examples for different grade levels. The resulting examples were then edited by the author. These examples also illustrate how humans can partner with AI to develop examples that, in turn, can be used to stimulate possibilities for helping students develop their own UxD projects.

encouraged students to be more open and accepting of others. The students also planned assemblies and invited guest speakers to talk about the importance of a sense of belonging in school. The students worked hard to make sure that their message was heard throughout the school and their efforts were greatly appreciated by their teachers and administrators. The impact of the club was impressive, as it helped create a more welcoming environment in the school.

The students were helped by their school's faculty and staff, who provided guidance and support throughout the project. They also partnered with local businesses and organizations to provide donations, which helped fund their activities. The positive impact of the club was and continues to be felt throughout the school community. It encouraged students, faculty, and staff to be more connected with each other and people from different backgrounds. The students also developed a plan to ensure that the club continues once they go on to middle school.

Middle School UxD Project Example

"Gardening for the Future"
Imagine a project designed by a group of 7th grade middle school students that was focused on addressing the need for healthy food options in their local community. The students identified that many people living nearby did not have access to fresh produce or nutritious meals, so they decided to create a vegetable garden on an unused piece of land near their school.

The students organized all aspects of this project, from designing the space and selecting which vegetables would be grown, sourcing materials like soil and compost needed for building the garden beds, as well as seeking out volunteers who were willing to help them with digging up the ground and planting seeds. They also set up a schedule where families could come and pick out freshly harvested fruits and veggies free of charge each week throughout summer months when most schools are closed for vacation.

To make sure the students had the knowledge necessary for implementing this project, the students arranged for local experts to provide weekly educational programs via Zoom about gardening basics along with activities such as painting flowerpots or making bird feeders. These efforts made it possible for many people around town to gain regular access to free and fresh produce thanks to generous donations from private businesses located in the community.

This initiative even provided younger children in the community with an opportunity to learn about sustainable farming methods under the guidance of 7th grade mentors and participating teachers. The students also developed a plan to involve 5th and 6th graders so the benefits of this project can continue long after the 7th graders move on to high school. The students are also working on a plan to scale-up the project so other communities elsewhere can implement it and benefit from it.

High School UxD Project Example

"UPLIFT"
Imagine a club designed by high school students called, *Uniting People for Local Improvement, Fostering Transformation* (UPLIFT). The goal of this club is to empower young people with the resources, knowledge, and skills needed to make an impactful change in and beyond their city. This club was started by a group of 11th and 12th grade students who partnered with non-profit organizations that specialize in providing assistance for those facing hardships.

Through these partnerships, students were able to identify areas of need and gain access not only to financial resources but also expert guidance from experienced professionals who could help guide them through implementation of their ideas into tangible projects around the city, such as building temporary shelters for homeless individuals or creating food banks within certain neighborhoods lacking adequate nutrition sources.

Another program initiated by project UPLIFT involved establishing virtual tutoring sessions for younger students in their community that was provided via Zoom. The virtual tutoring connected elementary and middle school students in need of academic assistance with retired teachers and other retired members of the community who were willing to share their wisdom, time, and knowledge about various topics ranging from supporting struggling readers and writers to providing math tutoring and science study sessions.

With donations from businesses both large and small within their surrounding areas along with other forms of support like volunteer work opportunities (provided by college alumni living nearby), project UPLIFT created positive ripples throughout multiple communities while developing valuable skills among its members.

The project has expanded to three other cities and is a highly popular elective club for juniors and seniors in high school. In fact, many students describe their experiences in project UPLIFT when applying for jobs and colleges. In this way, the club continues to make a positive and lasting impact on the high school students who participate in the club and numerous citizens in need who have been served by programs created by club UPLIFT.

CHAPTER 6

Seeing the Possible in Uncertainty

> Every block of stone has a statue inside it and it is the task of the sculptor to discover it.
> —Attributed to Michelangelo

> Merciless weeding of the ideational garden is absolutely essential to successful creativity.
> —Dean Simonton[1]

Once an Uncertainty x Design (UxD) learning experience has been planned, the next step is for students to generate actionable possibilities for resolving the uncertainty they face. Doing so is not a means to its own end. Rather, the idea is to help cultivate students' awareness, confidence, and ability to look for and act on possibilities to contribute to their own and others learning and lives.

Indeed, much like Michelangelo recognized that every block of stone has a statue inside, UxD learning experiences can help students identify possibilities in their encounters with uncertainty now and into their futures. And just like a gardener prunes weeds from the garden to allow plants to thrive, UxD learning experiences can also help students learn how to select, test-out, and cultivate the most promising possibilities for taking action.

The focus of this chapter is to describe how to support young people in exploring uncertainty for the production and selection of actionable possibilities. The chapter closes with Application 6, which provides a possibility thinking protocol that teachers can use to support students in producing and selecting possibilities for action.

Exploring Uncertainty for Possibilities

Learning how to produce and select possibilities for resolving unknowns in UxD learning experiences starts with a willingness to approach uncertainty

---

[1] Simonton, "Creativity as variation and selection: Some critical constraints."

with an *exploratory mindset*. An exploratory mindset is akin to what Michelangelo described in the opening quote of this chapter. Specifically, an exploratory mindset enables us to approach the unknown with the awareness that it can hold transformative possibilities.

Artists, architects, engineers, and other professionals who work with physical material approach the medium they are working with – be it stone, wood, recycled plastics, metal, or some combination thereof – with an exploratory mindset because they do not know for certain what the resulting product will turn out to be. This holds true even if they have a plan or model in mind for how they might work with material they are attempting to transform into something new.

As Christopher Bardt, a professor of architecture at the Rhode Island School of Design, has explained:

> when we manipulate actual material, wood for instance, it continually surprises and overturns the mental 'model' of wood [and] when a material doesn't fit our mind's assumptions – and it never does when we engage it – feelings such as doubt and belief emerge to be important ways to navigate the gulf between the mind's stable concepts of material and material's mutability.[2]

An exploratory mindset is necessary anytime students attempt to navigate the space between *what currently is* and *would could be*.[3] Consequently, when teachers introduce a UxD learning experience it will be important to encourage students to resist the temptation to quickly resolve uncertainty and instead spend time thinking about the problem or task in different ways (e.g., "Before you start, spend some time thinking about the problem and explore what you already know about it and how it might be viewed in different ways").

By slowing down the process and encouraging students to explore and discuss the problem or task with others, teachers can help to cultivate an exploratory mindset. Indeed, exploration often involves examining the features of a problem or task and looking for ways "into the uncertainty." This includes finding ways of getting a handle on the uncertainty.

Just like rock climbers explore the face of a cliff for finger and footholds, exploring uncertainty requires exploring the situation for affordances[4] that serve as possibilities for taking action. Exploring uncertainty is, therefore, similar to what creativity researchers call, *problem exploration*.[5] Problem

---

[2] Bardt, *Material and Mind*.   [3] Craft, "Possibility thinking: From what is to what might be."
[4] Gibson, "The ecological approach to visual perception."
[5] Problem exploration is an aspect of *problem finding* (see Chapter 2), which involves identifying, developing, and clarifying problems.

exploration represents a creative sensemaking process of exploring the problem space to clarify an ill-defined problem and identify new possibilities to pursue.[6]

In a now classic study,[7] art students were presented with an open-ended task that invited them to arrange a set of objects and then draw the arrangement. Students who spent more time exploring the uncertainty of the task before starting their drawings (e.g., handling more objects, examining the features of the objects) produced drawings that were rated as more creative than students who spent less time in exploration.

Prior research has also demonstrated that people who have a more exploratory mindset, what researchers call "openness to experience," tend to be able to generate more possibilities as compared to people who are not as open to new experiences.[8] Although openness has typically been viewed as a somewhat stable personality trait, there is evidence that our openness to new possibilities can grow whenever we take on new roles and through novel experiences.[9] Indeed, researchers[10] have documented how openness can be increased throughout the life span by taking on complex challenges, engaging in new cultural activities,[11] and experiencing different perspectives.[12]

Given that UxD learning experiences require students to take on complex challenges and engage with new and different perspectives, they represent a potentially powerful way to cultivate students' openness to new possibilities when facing uncertainties. Much like problem exploration is different from problem-solving, exploration of uncertainty is different from what students are typically asked to do when engaging in a learning task. This is why it is important that teachers prompt students to take more time exploring the problem space of the task because it can help them recognize different, interesting, and more viable possibilities.

Although recognition of the possible can come through exploration of uncertainty, it is also important to allow students to occasionally step away from the to-be-determined elements they face in UxD projects. This can be

---

[6] Runco & Chand, "Problem finding, evaluative thinking, and creativity"; Studer et al., "Evidence of problem exploration in creative designs."
[7] Csikszentmihalyi & Getzels, "Discovery-oriented behavior and the originality of creative products: A study with artists."
[8] McCrae, "Creativity, divergent thinking, and openness to experience."
[9] Roberts et al., "Personality development."
[10] Jackson et al., "Can an old dog learn (and want to experience) new tricks? Cognitive training increases openness to experience in older adults."
[11] Schwaba et al., "Openness to experience and culture-openness transactions across the lifespan."
[12] Sparkman et al., "Multicultural experiences reduce prejudice through personality shifts in Openness to Experience."

particularly beneficial when they start to feel stuck, frustrated, or incapable of recognizing possibilities for addressing the uncertainty they face.

Stepping away from uncertainty is not about giving up, but rather is about seeking out new ways to view the problem through reflection and by obtaining the perspectives, feedback, and support from others. Doing so can help students reset their view of the problem and, ultimately, recognize possibilities for taking action that they may have initially missed.

Indeed, stepping away to reflect on the uncertainty of a task and seeking feedback from others can be beneficial in generating possibilities because it enables students to approach the situation with "fresh eyes." The impressionist painter, Claude Monet, for instance, was famous for his ability to step away from mundane representations of scenes and, instead, approach them from a unique perspective that enabled him to see new possibilities for representing everyday landscapes with "visual freshness."[13]

Along similar lines, when students are encouraged to step away from a typical view of a problem and return to it with a sense of "visual freshness" they may be able to recognize actionable possibilities that they initially overlooked. Teachers can support this stepping-away process by letting students know in advance that they can step away when feeling stuck in order to step back into the problem from a different vantage point (e.g., "If you're feeling stuck, it's okay to take a break and discuss it with the larger group and then return to it once you have heard some different ways of thinking about it").

Teachers can also support this process by monitoring students' efforts (e.g., "I just want to check-in and see how things are going. I know it can be frustrating when you're feeling stuck, sometimes stepping away and talking to others can help you see the problem in a new way"). Teachers can then provide opportunities for students to seek out support and new perspectives from others to help them return to the problem with a renewed sense of the possible.

Producing *Actionable* Possibilities

Exploring uncertainty to produce possibilities aligns with what creativity researchers have described as "divergent thinking."[14] Divergent thinking involves generating multiple, unique, elaborate, and different types of possibilities. Although divergent thinking is similar to producing possibilities, in the context of UxD, generating possibilities differs in at least one important way: diverging from the actual has the aim of generating *actionable* possibilities.

---

[13] Heinrich, *Monet*.   [14] Runco & Acar, "Divergent thinking."

What Are Actionable Possibilities?

Actionable possibilities represent a form of action-oriented divergence, whereas divergent thinking is much broader and does not require that ideas produced are feasible, actionable, or transformative. Consequently, when helping students to produce possibilities in the context of UxD, there is an added requirement that the possibilities can be put into action.

Asking students, for instance, to come up with original ideas for a UxD project can meet the criterion of diverging from the actual but will not necessarily meet the criterion of producing possibilities that are feasible for action.[15] Similarly, students who are asked to come up with a project idea for addressing a problem at their school but simply copy a project presented two years ago would meet the actionable criterion, but would fail to meet the divergence criterion, because they are simply reproducing something that already exists.

It is therefore important that teachers help students recognize that both criteria are necessary when generating actionable possibilities in the context of UxD experiences. Unless students are specifically prompted to meet both criteria, they may not produce new *and* actionable possibilities. Indeed, some students may develop possibilities that turn out to be like existing solutions, whereas others generate highly original but impractical possibilities.

Teachers can help here by encouraging students to put a novel twist on something that lacks originality (e.g., "This project idea is similar to the example we discussed, how might you make it your own?") and, conversely, modify highly original ideas to make them more practical ("It's okay, at this point, if this idea doesn't seem like it will work ... let's keep it on the whiteboard and we can later see if we can modify it so that it can work for this project"). In all cases, educators can help students meet the two criteria of UxD possibility production by making sure that students' ideas diverge from what already exists *and* that those ideas are feasible for action.

How Can Students Generate Actionable Possibilities?

There are two broad ways[16] that students can generate possibilities that diverge from the actual. The first way is to try to *make the unfamiliar familiar* and the second way is to try to *make the familiar unfamiliar*. Once

---

[15] Ward & Kolomyts, "Creative cognition."
[16] Wagoner, "Commentary: Making the familiar unfamiliar"; Glăveanu, *The Possible: A Sociocultural Theory.*

Seeing the Possible in Uncertainty 101

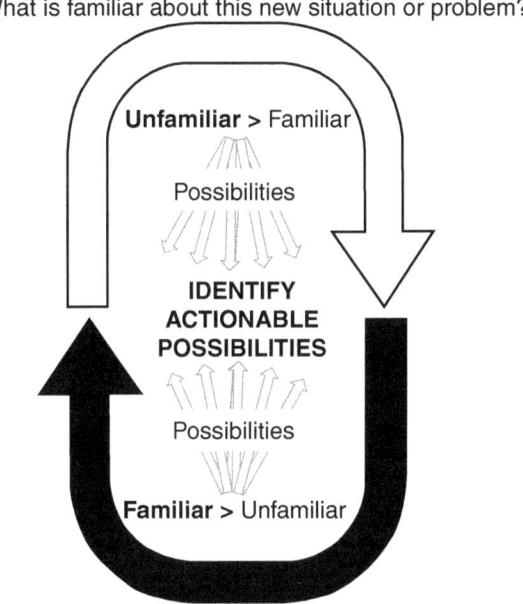

Figure 6.1 Making the familiar unfamiliar and the unfamiliar familiar

teachers understand these two heuristics, they can use them to help students generate actionable possibilities (see Figure 6.1).

As illustrated in Figure 6.1, students can produce possibilities by deviating from the actual to make the "familiar unfamiliar" or by making the "unfamiliar familiar." They can then work to refine the possibilities they generate to make sure they are feasible for action. Making the familiar unfamiliar to generate new possibilities can be prompted by posing questions such as: *What is a new or different way of thinking about this known problem or situation?*

This question prompts students to consider and challenge their assumptions about an existing problem or situation. A group of students working on the problem of bullying occurring in their school, for instance, might pose some *what if* possibilities that can help them see the problem in a new light:

> What if we view bullying in our school not as a problem, but an opportunity to build a stronger school community whereby students and teachers learn how to support each other in repairing relationships and cultivating an ethos of respect? What would that look like and how can we work toward actualizing this possibility?

Making the unfamiliar familiar is another way of generating actionable possibilities by exploring questions such as: *What is familiar about this new situation or problem?* This question prompts students to explore the unknown and find new ways of resolving uncertainty. "What if" thinking can be combined with "as if" thinking[17] to generate new possibilities by viewing the unknown about a problem or situation through the lens of the known.

Consider, for instance, a group of 8th grade students who want to address an emerging problem across different grade levels whereby 6th and 7th grade students are feeling isolated from each other:

> What if we viewed older and younger students across grade levels "as if" they are members of a family? We can then create different family groups of students across different grade levels who can briefly meet each week to check-in with each other, support each other throughout the school day, and even participate in collaborative activities and projects with each other and other family groups.

Taken together, these simple heuristics can be used in the face of uncertainty to generate powerfully productive and actionable possibilities. This is because these heuristics engage students' imagination, which moves them into possible futures whereby they can consider what currently is not the case, but could be the case.[18]

Indeed, these two heuristics animate students' imagination and thereby enable them to work in the space of the "unmade future"[19] and become "future makers."[20] When students are released from the certainty of existing beliefs, habits, and routines they can then generate new possibilities for action. This is the gift that the human imagination provides – it opens a new horizon of possibilities.

---

[17] Craft, "Possibility thinking: From what is to what might be"; Dahl & Moreau, "The influence and value of analogical thinking during new product ideation."
[18] Greene, *Releasing the Imagination: Essays on Education, the Arts, and Social Change.*
[19] Catmull & Wallace, *Creativity, Inc: Overcoming the Unseen Forces That Stand in the Way of True Inspiration.*
[20] Appadurai, *The Future as Cultural Fact.*

Selecting Possibilities

Once students have generated possibilities, they will then need to be supported in selecting those that seem most promising for resolving uncertainty. Selecting possibilities aligns with what creativity researchers call, *convergent thinking*.[21] Convergent thinking refers to the process by which we evaluate the merit of ideas and possibilities we have generated. Convergent thinking is necessary for creative problem-solving because it helps us select the ideas that seem to be the best suited for solving the problem at hand.

Convergent thinking also helps us slow down and carefully consider all the ideas we produce. This is particularly important for our most exciting ideas, because we may fail to adequately consider whether implementing those ideas could cause harm to ourselves and others (see also Chapter 8).[22] In practice, both possibility production and possibility selection are not only needed,[23] but often represent a tandem, reciprocal process.

Consequently, teaching students how to both produce and select possibilities is an important aim of UxD learning experiences. And more accomplished creators can do both. Indeed, researchers[24] have provided evidence demonstrating that people's ability to generate possibilities tends to be positively associated with their evaluative skills (i.e., selecting those that are most creative).

In the context of the UxD approach, this tandem, reciprocal process of producing and selecting possibilities is represented in Figure 6.2.

As illustrated in Figure 6.2, once students have generated a pool of possibilities they then attempt to narrow down that pool in an effort to select those that seem most viable for resolving the uncertainty they face in a UxD activity. This narrowing down process may result in modifying, revisiting, or even producing additional possibilities. Consequently, students will benefit from knowing that the selection process often involves a combination of *selection, pre-testing, refinement,* and even *identification of different possibilities* prior to acting.

Why go through this somewhat protracted process? Wouldn't it be more efficient to simply test out possibilities by applying them to a problem or task? One reason why it is important for students to learn how to go through the full possibility "production-selection" process is

---

[21] Cropley, "In praise of convergent thinking."   [22] Ibid.
[23] Hausman, *A Discourse on Novelty and Creation*.
[24] Guo et al., "Divergent thinking and evaluative skill: A meta-analysis."

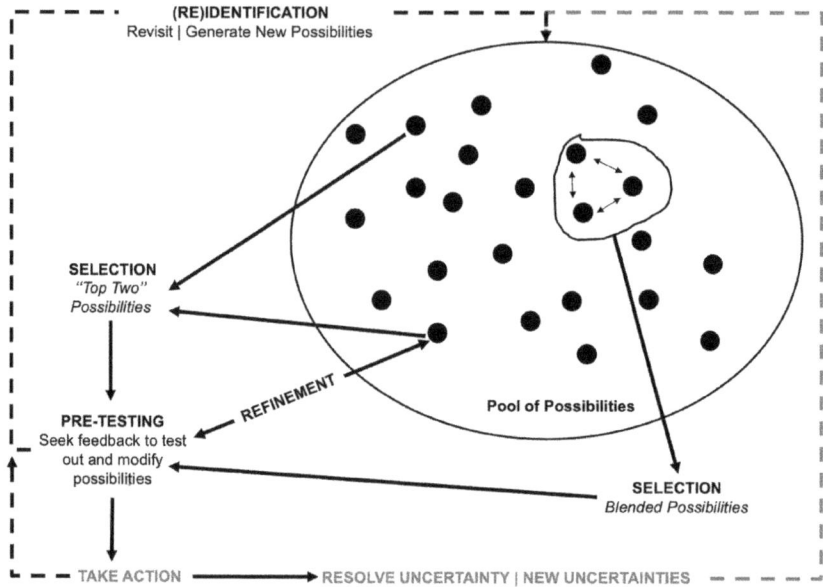

Figure 6.2 Selecting, refining, and reidentifying actionable possibilities

that it can benefit them in learning how to seek out *and* provide feedback, which is often beneficial for learning how to evaluate new and different possibilities.

Indeed, the findings from a large-scale study[25] demonstrated that evaluation accuracy is stronger when young people evaluate the creative ideas of other people who worked on a similar task. As the researchers on this study explained, these "results show that task exposure improves students' ability to accurately recognize creative and original ideas, and their ability to discriminate between highly feasible and unfeasible ideas."[26]

Moreover, there is also evidence that helping students develop their evaluative skills to provide feedback to others can increase their own capacity to produce novel and actionable possibilities. Consider, for instance, the findings from a study of undergraduate students[27] wherein researchers explored whether the process of having students provide

---

[25] van Broekhoven et al., "Creative idea forecasting: The effect of task exposure on idea evaluation."
[26] Ibid.
[27] Gibson & Mumford, "Evaluation, criticism, and creativity: Criticism content and effects on creative problem solving."

evaluative feedback would influence their own ability to generate new and useful ideas.

In the study, researchers asked students to develop an advertising campaign. Prior to asking students to prepare their advertising campaign students were presented with a set of candidate ideas and asked to critique those ideas. The researchers found that students who provided deep, specific, use-focused criticisms were, in turn, more creative in generating their own possibilities for the task. In this way, the researchers found that it was not about the *quantity* of critiques, but the *quality* of the critique. Indeed, simply producing many critiques was not beneficial and, in fact, was found to inhibit students' subsequent production of creative ideas.

The findings of this research suggest that teaching students how to provide a limited number of deep and focused critiques can be beneficial in supporting subsequent production of creative possibilities. In the context of UxD, students should thereby have the opportunity to receive quality critiques on their own ideas *and* have the opportunity to learn how to provide quality feedback to peers.

The somewhat protracted process of generating, selecting, testing, and revisiting possibilities for and with others likely will benefit students in both generating and identifying actionable possibilities. Figure 6.2 provides an illustration of this process, which represents a zoomed in or closer look at what occurs during the production and selection phase of UxD learning experiences.

More specifically, once a pool of possibilities has been generated, the next step is to select those that seem most viable for action. However, prior to taking action on these possibilities, they should first be "pre-tested" by seeking quality feedback from others. This, in turn, can result in the refinement of possibilities, returning to the pool of possibilities or even generating new ones. These various aspects of the selection process are briefly discussed in the sections that follow.

Selection of Possibilities

Once students are ready to select possibilities from those they have generated, teachers can support the process by providing them with some direction and guidance. Educators can, for instance, direct students to work alone or with others to identify two possibilities they believe are the most unique and feasible. The "top-two" approach has been used by creativity researchers to have people select what they believe are their most creative ideas. And there is evidence that creative people who have generated a pool of ideas and were then asked to select their top-two ideas had high levels of alignment with the ratings of external judges on those ideas.

More specifically, a study of university students[28] involved having students first generate possibilities and then select the top-two ideas that they thought were most creative (i.e., novel and useful). Next, a group of external judges rated the creativity of all the possibilities. The self-ratings of students were, on average, aligned with the judges' ratings. And this alignment was strongest in students who scored higher in openness to experience.

Although this "top-two" approach for selecting creative possibilities has been found to be linked with external ratings of creative ideas, there is also evidence that people do not always select the best ideas as compared to external judges[29] and sometimes under-rank their most creative ideas.[30] Therefore, the top-two idea approach might be too restrictive[31] when used for the purpose of identifying final possibilities for action. Consequently, the top-two approach should be viewed as a starting point for selecting actionable ideas in UxD learning experiences. Indeed, and as will be discussed in the next section, students likely will need to further refine or even identify new possibilities after "pre-testing" their top-two possibilities.

Finally, and as also illustrated in Figure 6.2, another way to support students in selecting possibilities is to invite them to try to combine several ideas into a "blended possibility." Doing so can result in a new, emergent possibility. Blended possibilities are often more novel and potentially more actionable than the initial ideas that were used to create it. Creativity researchers[32] call this process *conceptual combination* and have documented how it can result in new and creative outcomes. Here's an example of how this might look in a UxD project:

> A group of students have become aware of a local family who recently lost their home and are in immediate need of funds to move to a new housing arrangement. The students have been generating fundraising ideas for this family. And they have narrowed down ten possibilities to three that they believe they can implement in the time needed to do so. They want to try all three because it would raise more funds, but only have one weekend they can devote to the fundraiser. Their teacher encourages them to try to blend these different possibilities into a combined one. By doing so they

---

[28] Silvia, "Discernment and creativity: How well can people identify their most creative ideas."
[29] Zhu et al., "Creativity: Intrapersonal and interpersonal selection of creative ideas."
[30] Berg, "When silver is gold: Forecasting the potential creativity of initial ideas."
[31] Acar & Runco, "Divergent thinking: New methods, recent research, and extended theory."
[32] Ward & Kolomyts, "Creative cognition."

eventually land on the combined idea of a 'fundraising festival' whereby they can simultaneously implement all three ideas (and maybe even a few more).

Regardless of the approach taken to initially select possibilities, students should be encouraged to keep their options open and to test the possibilities they select by obtaining feedback from others prior to acting.

Pre-testing Possibilities

Once students have selected what they believe are their most viable possibilities, they should next *pre-test* them by seeking feedback from others. Doing so will help students *evaluate* the merit of the possibilities they selected based on the feedback they received. A key component of pre-testing possibilities is to anticipate potential roadblocks and other negative consequences of putting possibilities into action.[33]

Researchers have explained that when we generate possibilities, we tend to overlook important side effects or hazards because of "innovator bias."[34] Innovator bias refers to a tendency to focus on the positive aspects of the ideas we generate and downplay or fail to see any potentially negative consequences of implementing those possibilities. Fortunately, scholars have developed various strategies[35] to anticipate and identify potential downsides and thereby moderate overconfidence[36] and mitigate risks[37] prior to acting.

One way to address innovator bias is to have students imagine potential unintended consequences of acting on the possibilities they have generated. During pre-testing, educators can support this process by forming feedback groups and then invite students to present their ideas to each other. Next, teachers can guide students through the process of imagining that the possibility did not work out. They can then work together to discuss potential reasons why the ideas might fail if they were implemented and explore ways of strengthening their ideas prior to taking action (see Application 6).

---

[33] Seligman et al., "Navigating into the future or driven by the past"; Zhao, "What works may hurt: Side effects in education."
[34] Reece et al., "Enforcing pragmatic future-mindedness cures the innovator's bias."
[35] Klein, "Performing a project premortem"; Reece et al., "Enforcing pragmatic future-mindedness cures the innovator's bias."
[36] Veinott et al., "Evaluating the effectiveness of the premortem technique on plan confidence."
[37] Gallop et al., "How to catch a black swan: Measuring the benefits of the premortem technique for risk identification."

Finally, it is worth noting that students may not always need to go through the full selection process depicted in Figure 6.2. In some cases, it may be more efficient and effective for students to immediately apply a possible solution and evaluate whether it "works" rather than go through pre-testing. Students who, for instance, are tasked with generating different possibilities for how to solve a rather straightforward or well-defined problem could skip pre-testing and simply try out some possibilities.

However, in the case of UxD projects a more protracted production-selection process is often needed, because such designs are more complex and the stakes tend to be higher (e.g., requiring more time, effort, resources, and can have potentially unintended impacts on others).

Summary and Next Steps

In sum, developing students' confidence in their ability to produce actionable possibilities is a key goal of any UxD learning experience. Application 6 provides a protocol and examples of how teachers, peers, and other possibility thinking partners can support this goal. Once teachers have a working understanding of how to support students in selecting and producing possibilities, then they'll be in a better position to help support the kinds of students' self-beliefs necessary for acting on those possibilities, which is the focus of the next chapter.

APPLICATION 6 PRODUCING AND PRE-TESTING POSSIBILITIES

Overview

This application includes a possibility thinking protocol and a walk-through of the protocol to support teachers and students in generating and selecting actionable possibilities when designing and engaging in UxD learning. It can also be used for any situation that requires generating new possibilities for resolving uncertainty.

Application 6.1 Protocol for Producing and Pre-testing Possibilities

Purpose: The purpose of this protocol[38] is to provide structured and guided support to help students, colleagues, community members, or anyone generate, select, and pre-test actionable possibilities prior to taking action.

Group Size: 2 to 100+

Process

Part I: What If? | Generating and Selecting Possibilities

1. Introduction: The facilitator briefly describes the purpose of the protocol and provides a brief overview of the process. Then an individual or team describes uncertainty they are facing with respect to a challenge, problem, or topic that they are working on in an effort to generate actionable possibilities for resolving that uncertainty. Everyone else serves as "possibility partners" and will help the presenter challenge assumptions, generate, select, and pre-test possibilities for taking action to resolve the uncertainty they face.
2. Briefly describe the problem (i.e., the uncertainty you are facing): The presenter (an individual or representative of a team) concisely describes the uncertainty they are facing with respect to some specific challenge, project, task, or problem they are working on (e.g., "We want to address the problem of social isolation in our school";

---

[38] Adapted from Beghetto, "Taking beautiful risks in education."

"We want to help children in our community who cannot afford to purchase new clothing at the start of each school year.")

3. Clarifying Questions: The "possibility partners" ask any clarifying questions they have about the challenge, problem, or issue presented. The clarifying questions should be brief and specific aimed at better understanding the nature of the problem and uncertainty encountered. No solutions or ideas for addressing the uncertainty should be provided at this time. The presenter provides brief clarification.

4. "What if" | "As If" possibilities: "Possibility partners" then provide as many new and different ways of thinking about the problem, or potential ways to respond, as they can. Preface all suggestions with "*What if...?*" or "It is *as if...*" to signal that this is just a possibility to be considered. The possibilities should encourage the presenter and everyone to challenge their assumptions about the problem or issue. The facilitator will monitor and remind participants to preface all suggestions with "*What if*" and "*As if.*"

   Important Note: During this step, the presenter listens quietly without interrupting or clarifying, perhaps taking notes. The goal is for the presenter to take in as many different perspectives as possible without short-circuiting the process with interruptions.

5. Select Actionable Possibilities. Once the "possibility partners" have provided multiple possibilities for the presenter(s) to consider, then the facilitator will ask the presenter(s) to reflect on all the possibilities presented and select one or two of the most promising and actionable ones. The presenter then briefly shares with the group the possibility selected and initial steps that can be taken to put this possibility into action.

Part II: What If Not? | Pre-testing Possibilities

6. Prior to Taking Action, Imagine How It Might Fail: The facilitator now asks the group to imagine that implementing the idea has failed. The purpose of doing so is to help the individual (or team) anticipate and proactively address potential hazards of implementing a project idea or action, or problems likely to arise.

7. Why Did the Possibility Fail?: Everyone in the group individually imagines and describes at least one reason why taking action on the possibility failed. Any clarifications can be requested and provided at this stage.

8. Proactively Address Anticipated Setbacks: In this step, the group again uses "What if?" questions to explore possibilities for proactively addressing these anticipated challenges and setbacks. This process continues until each reason has been read aloud and participants have shared ideas for addressing it. The facilitator can note similarities between concerns (and unique concerns) and challenges brought up frequently.
9. Reflection and Next Steps for Taking Action: The facilitator guides a discussion of what the group learned from this process, summarizes what was learned, and outlines next steps for the group (such as planning concrete actions to address one or two of the setbacks or even engaging in another round of possibility thinking to address a new challenge that emerged during discussion).

Application 6.2   Example Walk-Through of the Protocol

Group Size: *Presenter* (author) and *AI Possibility Partner*. This example highlights how one human working in collaboration with OpenAI's GTP-3 model can use this protocol to generate and pre-test possibilities.

Resulting Dialogue

Part I: Producing Possibilities
Describe the Problem

PRESENTER: We want to help children in our community who cannot afford to purchase new clothing at the start of each school year. Do you have any clarifying questions you would like to ask about this project?

Clarifying Questions
AI-Possibility Partner
- How many children in the community require assistance with purchasing new clothing for school?
- What type of clothing is typically needed by these children (e.g., shirts, pants, shoes)?
- Are there any existing organizations or programs that already provide assistance to families in need of support for back-to-school shopping?
- Is this project focused on providing financial resources directly to families or facilitating donations from other sources like local businesses and/or individuals?

Clarification

PRESENTER: These are good questions, here's our response: We have heard that there are at least fifty students who can benefit from this program. Families would benefit from all types of clothing (shirts, pants, shoes). There are some organizations that provide used clothing to the community, but not always what families need. The project is focused on finding out what specific clothing is needed and providing the clothing to families. This will require donations.

Can you now provide us with some "what ifs?" or "as if" analogies for the problem that can serve as possibilities for considering how we might address this problem? Can you also help us challenge some assumptions we might have about this problem?

"What If" and "As If" Possibilities
AI Possibility Partner
What If
- ... the most effective way to help these children get new clothing is through connecting them with local businesses for discounted goods?
- ... we could mobilize the community by creating an online platform where people can donate directly to families in need of support, or create awareness campaigns that start conversations about why it's important to provide families access at the start of each school year?
- ... we partner up with thrift shops that can help meet the specific needs of families?"

Challenging Assumptions
- What if instead of providing financial resources ourselves, we enlisted our community members (local business owners, individuals, etc.) to facilitate donations so that there would be enough available funds for all fifty students' back-to-school shopping needs?
- What if traditional retail shops and chain department stores partnered up with us and offered discounts?

Selection of Actionable Possibilities and First Steps

PRESENTER: We like the idea of partnering with the community to get donations. As a first step, we can reach out to some retail shops in our community and explore their interest and willingness to participate. Are there any other initial steps we can take?

AI POSSIBILITY PARTNER: Yes, we can start to research organizations and local businesses that have shown interest in partnering with projects such as this one. We should also develop a timeline for the project including when donations will be accepted and distributed. We can also begin spreading information about our effort through social media platforms.

Finally, it would be beneficial to determine what other resources are available within the community that may complement or enhance our efforts (other charities, funding sources). This will help us ensure that all children who need assistance receive support at the beginning of each school year.

Part II: What If Not? | Pre-testing the Selected Possibilities
Imagining the Project Fails

PRESENTER: Thank you, these sound like good first steps. Let's imagine that we move forward with this project, but it is a failure. What are some reasons why it failed?

Reasons Why the Project Might Fail

AI POSSIBILITY PARTNER: Some possible reasons why the project may fail could include a lack of resources or funding, insufficient volunteer support needed to carry out activities related to the project, difficulty in connecting with and reaching families who need assistance and identifying local businesses willing to participate.

Additionally, if there isn't enough outreach done on social media channels or through other communication outlets (e.g., newspapers), then potential donors may not be aware of our effort, and this can hinder its success as well. Finally, unanticipated changes in external factors that are beyond our control such as an economic recession could also lead to decreased donations which would further impede progress.

Proactively Addressing Setbacks

PRESENTER: What can we do to proactively address these potential setbacks before they happen?

AI POSSIBILITY PARTNER: Here are some ideas to proactively address these potential setbacks:
- Develop a detailed budget plan with multiple funding sources to ensure that there are enough resources available for the project.
- Establish and maintain consistent communication channels to keep volunteers informed of upcoming tasks they can help contribute toward in order to support the initiative's progress.
- Reach out through various community networks such as schools or churches so we can identify families who need assistance and connect them with our program's offerings if appropriate/necessary.

- Partner up with local businesses ahead of time on promotional activities which could be beneficial for both parties involved during unexpected events. Develop contingency plans for what to do if something unexpected happens.

Elaboration and Next Steps

AUTHOR: In addition to these ideas, what other things might we want to consider so that our project is a success?

AI POSSIBILITY PARTNER: Some other considerations include setting measurable goals with clear objectives and timelines for the project, creating quality assurance protocols to ensure that donated clothing is appropriate both in terms of size/style as well as condition.

Moreover, developing a strategy which considers unanticipated scenarios, such as last-minute donations from individual donors who may want their contributions to remain anonymous.

Reflection

PRESENTER: Thank you, this has been helpful in considering possibilities, potential setbacks, and potential first steps. Finally, let's reflect on what we learned from engaging in this process. What did you learn from this process?

AI POSSIBILITY PARTNER: I have learned that there are many factors to consider when planning a project, especially those related to the quality and availability of resources. Additionally, I've come away with an understanding that successful projects often involve collaboration from various stakeholders (businesses, individuals, etc.) as well as include strategies for addressing unexpected scenarios in order to ensure that desired outcomes can be achieved. Moreover, being proactive instead of reactive is key so one can identify potential setbacks before they occur and put plans into place which could help prevent them from materializing or reduce their impact if they do arise.

CHAPTER 7

To Act or Not to Act

> Self-belief does not necessarily ensure success, but self-disbelief assuredly spawns failure.
> —Albert Bandura[1]

> Alone we can do so little. Together we can do so much.
> —Helen Keller[2]

Why do some people take action in the face of uncertainty whereas others do not? One reason is because they believe they can resolve the uncertainty they face. If they do not, then they likely will avoid taking action or defer action to others.[3] In this way, two people encountering the same type of uncertainty may react to it in very different ways. This is somewhat obvious.

What is less obvious, however, is what goes into our judgments about whether the uncertainty is actionable and, most importantly, whether we will *actually* take and sustain action on new possibilities to resolve the uncertainty we face. There are countless examples that highlight the difference between a desire to act in the face of uncertainty and actually putting forth and sustaining the effort to do so. New Year's resolutions serve as a common example.

Many of us approach each new year with a spirit of the possible. Although we may be uncertain about what the new year might hold for us, we view it as an opportunity to make some positive and lasting change in our lives (ranging from improving our health to other forms of self-improvement). We thereby resolve to make a change. But resolving to do something and doing it actually are two different things.[4] Indeed, how many of us actually follow through on our resolutions?

---

[1] Bandura, *Self-Efficacy: The Exercise of Control.*
[2] Lash, *Helen and Teacher: The Story of Helen Keller and Anne Sullivan Macy.*
[3] Beghetto, "How times of crisis serve as a catalyst for creative action: An agentic perspective."
[4] Argyris & Schon, *Theory in Practice: Increasing Professional Effectiveness.*

There are many factors that go into whether people will take action and sustain effort when implementing new possibilities, including New Year's resolutions. Researchers who have looked into whether people are successful in making sustainable changes based on their New Year's resolutions have found that people who have confidence in making such changes are more likely to be successful over time than those who lack confidence.[5]

In addition to confidence beliefs, researchers have found that people who adopt approach-oriented goals for their resolutions (e.g., improve physical health) versus avoidance-oriented goals (i.e., stop using tobacco) and received social support along the way also tended to report being more successful making and sustaining changes over time (i.e., one year after the resolution).[6]

In short, people's confidence in their ability to be successful when taking positive action *and* the support they receive when attempting to do so matters.[7] The same can be said for students who have generated possibilities in the context of UxD learning experiences. Much like taking sustainable action on New Year's resolutions, students can also be supported in cultivating the self-beliefs and efforts necessary for putting the possibilities they generate into action, which is the aim of this chapter.

Understanding Thresholds of Action

In the context of UxD learning experiences, the kinds of problems and tasks that young people face can be thought of as having a threshold of *actionable uncertainty*.[8] Actionable uncertainty refers to the level of uncertainty whereby people believe they can take and sustain action. Judgments about whether uncertainty is actionable are subjective and dynamic. And they become activated in students when they encounter and attempt to work through the to-be-determined elements of UxD learning experiences.

These judgments are based, in part, on students' self-beliefs (i.e., confidence in being successful, seeing value in taking action, and willingness to take the risks necessary for action) and, in part, on the social support students receive. Social support for students can come in many forms, including everything from perceiving their teachers as being supportive of their efforts to receiving actual assistance from peers, teachers, skilled professionals, and sociocultural tools (e.g., relevant materials, resources, and technologies).

---

[5] Norcross et al., "*Auld lang Syne*: Success predictors, change processes, and self-reported outcomes of New Year's resolvers and nonresolvers."
[6] Oscarsson et al., "A large-scale experiment on New Year's resolutions: Approach-oriented goals are more successful than avoidance-oriented goals."
[7] Bandura, *Self-Efficacy: The Exercise of Control.*   [8] Beghetto, "Uncertainty."

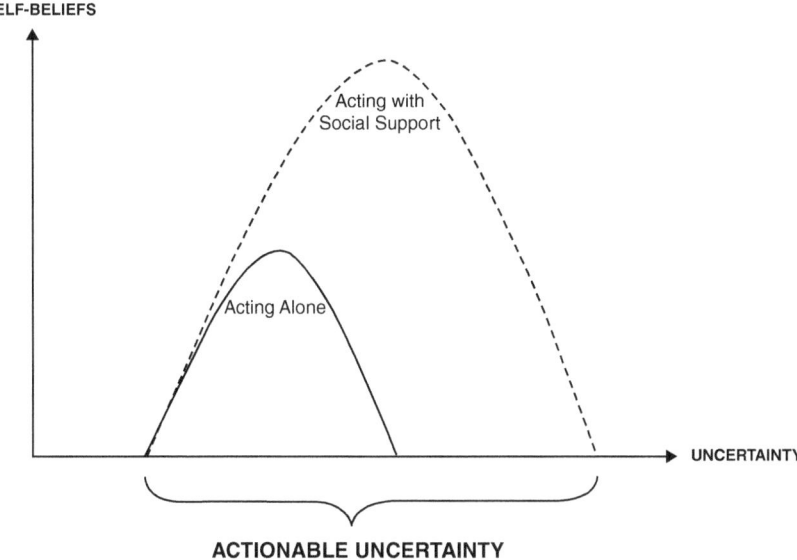

Figure 7.1 Thresholds of action under uncertainty

Figure 7.1 provides a model that posits different thresholds of actionable uncertainty for students working alone and students working with social supports.

The model depicted in Figure 7.1 illustrates a range of uncertainty whereby students believe they can (and cannot) take new forms of action. At very low levels of uncertainty, there is no need for students to act in new and different ways, because the uncertainty is easily resolvable with more routine thought and behavior. A student who is working through a social studies worksheet might, for instance, not remember a date of a historical event (low level of uncertainty) but can simply look it up in the textbook or Google it.

As uncertainty increases, the need to think and act in new ways also increases. Students who, for instance, want to help members of an unincorporated community experiencing chronic water shortages would need to come up with a variety of different and novel possibilities for how they might help. Given that this problem is quite complex (i.e., high levels of uncertainty), whether students believe they could do something about this problem is based, in part, on their self-beliefs and whether they are acting alone or acting with the support of others.

When students are acting alone in the face of uncertainty, there is a peak or maximum threshold whereby they believe they can take action (e.g., "I can solve this kind of problem, even though it is very complex"). The optimal individual level of tension is depicted as the peak of the "acting alone" curve in Figure 7.1. This level is optimal because it is the most likely to result in students acting in the face of uncertainty ("I'm not sure how to do this, but I can figure it out").

Scholars have similarly described how we are most likely to be moved into exploratory behaviors and actions when we arrive at an optimal level of arousal preference.[9] In the context of UxD, the optimal level of actionable uncertainty is dynamic and will, thereby, vary across and within situations, students, and tasks.

As the intensity of uncertainty increases beyond the peak level for individual students, we can expect that they will no longer believe they can resolve the uncertainty on their own (e.g., "I thought I could do this project, but it is getting too complex for me to do"). According to the model presented in Figure 7.1, this threshold (i.e., the point where a student feels the task is too uncertain to handle) can be increased if the student receives social support.

When acting with others, the model posits that students' range of actionable uncertainty likely will expand to include situations and tasks characterized by higher levels of uncertainty (e.g., "This project is too complex for me to do on my own, but I can do it if I get some help.").

In this way, opportunities to collaborate with more skilled others represents one of the most important forms of support that can help structure uncertainty and significantly expand the range of what students perceive as actionable (see Figure 7.1).

Indeed, creativity scholars and educational researchers have long recognized the importance of the role collaboration can play in expanding the horizons of what is possible in their learning, development, and when taking creative action.[10] Lev Vygotsky's psychological concept of the *zone of proximal development*[11] is one of the best-known examples of this way of thinking. The zone of proximal development refers to

> the distance between the actual developmental level as determined by independent problem solving and the level of potential development as

---

[9] Gustafsson, "How can contextual variables influence creative thinking? Contributions from the optimal-level of arousal model."
[10] Jefferson & Anderson, *Transforming Schools: Creativity, Critical Reflection, Communication, Collaboration*; Moran & John-Steiner, "How collaboration in creative work impacts identity and motivation."
[11] Vygotsky & Cole, "Mind and society: Development of higher psychological processes."

determined through problem solving under adult guidance or in collaboration with more capable peers.

Teachers can draw on this general line of thinking to help students expand what they believe they are capable of doing in the context of UxD learning experiences. Indeed, when students make judgments about whether the uncertainty they face is actionable, their appraisals are governed by their own self-beliefs and thereby they may focus only on what they are capable of doing alone.

Educators can therefore help students move beyond this more restricted view by allowing them to work with peers and more skilled others. Doing so can expand the range of what students view as actionable. Although collaboration can increase the range of actionable uncertainty, there are still limits. Indeed, there is also an upper limit or optimal level for collaborative action (see Figure 7.1).

Once the uncertainty exceeds this level, students may not be willing or able to take action on possibilities, regardless of their beliefs or amount of collaboration and support they receive ("I thought we could do this, but this project is more complex than we initially thought. I don't think we can do this, no matter who helps us!") In such cases, educators can help students readjust their goals and efforts (e.g., "What if your team scales the project back a bit and focuses instead on just one aspect? You might want to try something different, given the complexity of this project and limited time and resources you have available ...").

In other cases, providing too much structure and support can, somewhat ironically, reduce or eliminate the need for students to take creative action (e.g., "We couldn't come up with a good idea for the science experiment, but the other science teacher told us about one we can do and showed us a step-by-step process for how to conduct the experiment"). When this happens, increasing uncertainty will be needed to motivate creative action (e.g., "Ok that's a good example, but you still need to come up with your own idea for an experiment ... let's try to come up with some different ideas that you may be interested in ..."). In this way, there is an upper and lower limit to what students will view as actionable whether they are acting alone or with the support of others.

Finally, it is worth noting that students' perceptions of what is (and is not) actionable may not be accurate.[12] In some cases, they may

---

[12] Kaufman & Beghetto, "In praise of Clark Kent: Creative metacognition and the importance of teaching kids when (not) to be creative."

underestimate their abilities and thereby will need encouragement and support to put forth and sustain effort. In other cases, they may overestimate their capabilities to engage with and resolve uncertainty and would benefit from feedback and reflection on how to best move forward.

The only way to find out is for students to take action, monitor their progress, seek help when needed, and make any needed adjustments. Doing so can result in students' developing more accurate self-beliefs, learning how to obtain additional assistance, and even learning when it may be best to stop pursuing one line of action in pursuit of a more viable direction. At this point, it may be helpful to take a closer look at the kinds of students' self-beliefs and social supports that play a role in determining whether students will view the uncertainty of UxD learning experiences as actionable.

A Closer Look at Self-Beliefs

Students' self-beliefs become activated whenever they approach, engage with, and sustain effort on a task. Students' beliefs, relevant for UxD learning experiences, can be thought of as being represented in at least three interrelated questions:

- *Can I do this?* (Confidence beliefs)
- *Why should I do this?* (Perceived value beliefs), and
- *Am I willing to do this?* (Risk-taking beliefs)

Although these questions may seem simple or straightforward, upon closer inspection we will see that they reflect agentic beliefs, which refer to students' subjective judgments (or self-beliefs) that influence whether they are willing to take creative (i.e., new and personally meaningful) action in a particular situation and at particular point in time.[13] Students' agentic beliefs become activated across the various time points of a UxD learning experience (i.e., before engagement, during engagement, and following engagement).

Consequently, students' agentic beliefs play a central role in UxD learning experiences because the UxD approach invites students to exercise their own agency, rather than simply conform to what is expected and how it is expected. As has been discussed, the UxD approach puts students in the driver's seat of their learning such that they are invited to make their own decisions about how to approach the uncertainties they face.

---

[13] Karwowski & Kaufman, *The Creative Self: Effect of Beliefs, Self-Efficacy, Mindset, and Identity*.

This doesn't mean that students' self-beliefs cannot or should not be supported, rather it highlights the importance of educators understanding the nature of these kinds of beliefs so that they *can be* supported. Indeed, research that has examined the role of agentic beliefs in moving from creative potential to creative action can offer useful insights for teachers.

For instance, the Creative Behavior as Agentic Action framework (CBAA)[14] offers a particularly promising way to support the cultivation of the self-beliefs reflected in the agentic questions posed above. In accordance with this model, one way to think about students engaging with uncertainty in the context of UxD learning experiences is to recognize that doing so is a creative act,[15] because it requires students to think and act in new ways. And it is not known, in advance, whether their new thoughts or actions will successfully resolve the uncertainty they face.

Consequently, whenever students face uncertainty in UxD learning experiences, the CBAA framework would posit that they will decide whether to put forth and sustain effort based, in part, on whether they have confidence in their ability to be successful (i.e., Can I do this?), whether they see value in taking action (e.g., Why should I do this?), and whether they are willing to take the risks necessary to do so (i.e., Will I do this?).

Can I Do This?

When viewed from the vantage point of the CBAA framework, students' confidence in their ability to take action in the face of uncertainty can be thought of as having two facets.[16] The first is a more *stable* facet based largely on past experiences (e.g., "I am good at resolving uncertainties I face"; "I enjoy tackling problems that don't have clear answers"). The second is a more *dynamic* facet focused on impending performance (e.g., "I'm confident that I can come up with a new problem to solve for this specific project," "I am confident I can come up with a lot of different ways to solve this particular problem").

The more stable facet reflects students' general or "walking around" confidence in their ability to think and act in new ways to resolve uncertainty. This stable facet develops over time and through students'

---

[14] Karwowski & Beghetto, "Creative behavior as agentic action"; Beghetto et al., "Intellectual risk taking: A moderating link between creative confidence and creative behavior?"
[15] Beghetto, "There is no creativity without uncertainty: Dubito ergo creo."
[16] Beghetto & Karwowski, "Toward untangling creative self-beliefs."

experiences engaging with and successfully working through uncertainties in UxD learning experiences and everyday life.

The CBAA model posits a variety of dynamic and situational factors[17] that can influence students' confidence to resolve uncertainty, including students' physiological state, the specific nature of the uncertainty students face in a task, and social influences. In fact, when students face uncertainty in a particular task, at a particular time, and in a particular context then the more dynamic facet of their confidence beliefs come "on-line." Consequently, even students who tend to be generally confident in their ability to engage with uncertainty may (and likely will) come across situations, problems, and tasks in UxD learning experience whereby they lack confidence (e.g., "I don't think I can do this ...") and will benefit from social support.

As mentioned, students' confidence can change from when they first engage in the uncertainty of a task, during the various points of the task, and at the end of a task.[18] Application 7 provides ways of monitoring agentic beliefs across these various points of a UxD learning experience. At this point, however, it is important to first consider how students' confidence beliefs work in concert with their perceived value beliefs (i.e., "Why should I do this?") and their willingness to take creative risks (i.e., "Will I do this?").

Why Should I Do This?

Although healthy confidence beliefs seem to be a necessary component in determining whether students will take action in the face of uncertainty, they are not sufficient. Even if students feel confident in their ability to engage with and resolve uncertainty, they likely will not do so unless they also see the value in taking action (e.g., "I have some ideas that can help raise funds for the skatepark my peers are developing, but I don't like skateboarding and really don't see the point in building a skatepark, so I'm not going to share my ideas.").

This belief is reflected in the agentic question, "Why should I do this?" The way in which students respond to this question reflects their beliefs about the perceived value, merit, and worth of engaging with the uncertainty of a UxD design in relation to their broader goals and sense of self. The CBAA framework describes how perceived value works in conjunction with confidence in determining whether to take action in the face of

---

[17] Bandura, *Self-Efficacy: The Exercise of Control*.
[18] Karwowski et al., "Toward dynamizing the measurement of creative confidence beliefs."

uncertainty. More specifically, the CBAA framework draws on an *expectancy x value* approach.[19]

The expectancy x value approach would predict that any time students encounter uncertainty they will make an appraisal about whether that uncertainty is actionable based on their expectation that they can be successful resolving it ("I'm confident I can help solve this problem facing my community") *and* whether they see value in doing so ("I want to do this because it can help people in my community").

Given that this is a multiplicative relationship, even if students believe they can take action, they likely will avoid doing so in the face of uncertainty if they don't see why they should expend the effort. Similarly, if students see the value in taking action, but don't have the confidence in their ability to successfully resolve the uncertainty they face, then they likely will also avoid doing so. Students need to be able to affirmatively address both agentic questions of "Can I do this?" and "Should I do this?" in order to be in a position to take and sustain action in UxD designs.

In a series of three studies, my colleague Maciej Karwowski and I provided support for this prediction.[20] Specifically, we found that the link between people's potential to think and act in new ways and their engagement in creative activities and achievements was predicted by creative confidence and moderated by valuing creative action. These findings indicate that students need both confidence in their ability to act and see the value in doing so in order to put forth and sustain effort when facing uncertainty in UxD learning experiences.

Am I Willing to Do This?

Finally, in addition to students having confidence in their ability to act on possibilities and see the value in doing so, the CBAA framework posits that students also need to be willing to take the creative risks necessary to put their possibilities into action. More specifically, taking action in the face of uncertainty is risky because it is not possible to know, in advance, whether doing so will be successful.

Consequently, students' willingness to act on possibilities is informed by whether they judge the perceived benefits of taking action ("If I share my

---

[19] Eccles & Wigfield, "In the mind of the actor: The structure of adolescents' achievement task values and expectancy-related beliefs."
[20] Karwowski & Beghetto, "Creative behavior as agentic action."

idea, then I think it will help this project be a success") as outweighing the perceived costs ("If I share my idea, some of the older students might laugh at me or think I'm not as smart as them").

Although this cost-benefit analysis may seem somewhat straightforward, in practice, these judgments are not based on cold, objective logic. Rather, these judgments are highly subjective, and the prospect of failure can elicit a wide range of emotional and sociopsychological[21] considerations (e.g., potential of experiencing embarrassment, shame, concerns of letting ourselves and others down, fear of being laughed at by others, looking less competent than others, and so on).

Not surprisingly, researchers who have examined decision-making under states of uncertainty have documented that people tend to be risk averse, or more specifically, loss averse. This, in turn, can impede reasoning,[22] which is often reflected in a "negativity bias,"[23] whereby we tend to give more weight to potentially negative outcomes, even if the positive outcomes are equally likely or otherwise might be worth the risk.

Awareness of these challenges take on particular importance in the context of UxD learning experiences, because even if students have the confidence to take action and the risks are largely beneficial, they may still be reluctant to do so. Indeed, prior research has demonstrated that students who anticipate negative consequences from sharing their unique ideas were less likely to be interested in and less likely to put forth effort in a school-based creativity challenge.[24] Therefore, part of supporting students in developing their willingness to take a "leap of faith" and take beneficial risks in UxD learning experiences requires anticipating, recognizing, and proactively supporting students in working through these concerns.

Another, equally important, part of supporting students in deciding whether engaging in UxD learning experiences is worth the risk is to help them see beyond themselves and consider the potential costs and benefits to others. This reflects the transformative ethos of UxD learning designs, whereby the cost-benefit analysis is not simply transactional ("What will I get out of this?") but expanded to consider the impact on others ("How might my actions impact others?").

---

[21] Beghetto & Dilley, "Creative aspirations or pipe dreams? Toward understanding creative mortification in children and adolescents"; Beghetto & McBain, *My Favorite Failure*.
[22] Kahneman & Tversky, "Prospect theory: An analysis of decision under risk."
[23] Baumeister et al., "Bad is stronger than good."
[24] Ivcevic & Hoffmann, "The creativity dare: Attitudes toward creativity and prediction of creative behavior in school."

In sum, UxD experiences require students to exercise their agency throughout the entire process. This starts with encountering uncertainty and generating actionable possibilities, and extends to exerting effort to resolve uncertainty. And their beliefs play a central role in whether they think they can, should, and will take and sustain effort in the face of uncertainty.

Although agentic beliefs will vary across students and situations, what remains constant is that all students will likely need and benefit from timely social support from their teachers and skilled others. These supports will help them navigate critical moments in UxD learning experiences.

Social Support

Whether it be generating and testing out possibilities, receiving feedback on possibilities, viewing challenges and setbacks in a new light, obtaining just-in-time assistance, or having someone who encourages and helps holds us accountable, most (if not all) of us can benefit from social support when acting in the face of uncertainty. The same can be said for students as they work through the entire UxD learning process.

Although the ideas and applications presented in the previous chapters provide various ways that educators can provide social support to students when they encounter and attempt to resolve uncertainty, there are various other social supports that students may need and benefit from throughout the UxD process. These additional social supports include *establishing flexible UxD agreements; anticipating and preparing for failure and setbacks;* and *monitoring students' agentic beliefs and self-regulation strategies.* Each will be discussed in turn.

Establishing Flexible UxD Agreements

Given that UxD experiences represent a departure from what many students (and educators) are used to in school, it can be helpful to establish agreements that can help structure how students and teachers approach and work together.[25] The agreements should be flexible (rather than fixed), so they can be modified and tailored to specific contexts, situations, and groups. Students should also be involved in the process of establishing,

---

[25] Littleton & Mercer, "Interthinking: Putting talk to work."

Table 7.1 *Example agreements across phases of UxD activities*

Phase of UxD Activities	Younger Students	Older Students
When encountering uncertainty	"We agree to ... - try new things, - ask for help, and - be confident when facing something that we don't know how to do yet."	"We agree to ... - approach uncertain situations with a spirit of exploration and curiosity, and - remain open to different perspectives and solutions."
When producing and selecting possibilities	"We agree to ... - work together and - help each other come up with the best idea."	"We agree to ... - think critically, and - draw on our diverse backgrounds and experiences to come up with the most effective solutions."
When acting on possibilities	"We agree to ... - act on the ideas we come up with and - be kind to each other when doing it."	"We agree to ... - take action on the solutions we come up with, and - provide support and feedback to each other in the process."
When monitoring progress and impact	"We agree to ... - talk to others about how we are doing and - think about how what we do might make other people feel."	"We agree to ... - regularly check in on our progress and - assess the impact our decisions may have on others."

monitoring, and modifying agreements to ensure that students feel vested in them and supported by them.

Table 7.1 provides example agreements (written in the language of younger and older students), arranged under various phases of UxD learning experiences.[26] The example agreements can serve as starting points for helping educators and students develop their own agreements that are tailored to their context (e.g., modifying language to make it more accessible, relevant, and understandable for a particular group, situation, or task).

Again, the agreements in Table 7.1 are just examples which can be modified and tailored to specific groups of students in particular projects

---

[26] The examples in Table 7.1 were generated with the assistance of OpenAI's playground using a GPT model.

and contexts. The point here is that establishing agreements plays an important role in supporting students' efforts throughout the entire UxD process. Ultimately, UxD agreements have the aim of developing students' confidence and competence in their abilities to productively engage with uncertainty in and beyond UxD learning experiences.

Anticipating and Preparing for Failure and Setbacks

In addition to establishing UxD agreements, another key social support involves helping students anticipate and prepare for failures and setbacks when engaging in UxD projects. This should be done at the outset of any new UxD learning experience and revisited throughout the process. A promising approach for doing so is to have educators and students share brief stories of their favorite failures.

Favorite failure narratives have the goal of "naturalizing" the process of failure. This includes going beyond empty slogans (e.g., "Learn from your mistakes," "Fail forward," and "Have grit") and toward anticipating the negative emotions that can come with failure and how working through setbacks can lead to learning and growth. The favorite failure narrative framework[27] is based on the following five questions:

1. *Think about a time you tried something new or important and it didn't work out? What happened?* This question can be tailored to a specific type of situation or academic subject area (e.g., working on a group project, a creative science project that failed, designing your own outfit for a school dance that failed, and so on).
2. *How did you feel when it happened?* This question helps move beyond slogans and platitudes (e.g., "failure is the friend of learning") and highlights the emotional dimension of failure, including negative emotions.
3. *What did you learn from that situation?* The aim of this question is to highlight what was learned from this experience. It can be something that was learned at that moment, upon later reflection, or some combination thereof.
4. *What did you learn about yourself?* This is an important question that speaks to self-learning and how this setback influenced you as a person and your approach to taking creative risks in learning and life.

---

[27] Beghetto & McBain, *My Favorite Failure*.

5. *Why is this your favorite failure?* Finally, this question helps to reframe failure in a more generative light – seeing difficult challenges and emotionally painful setbacks as opportunities for personal growth.

When introducing favorite failures to students, teachers should start by sharing one (or more) brief stories of their own favorite failures. Doing so can go a long way in modeling how setbacks can be expected in learning and life, but also generative of new possibilities. Sharing favorite failures and inviting others to do so (in small groups or whole groups) can also help to build a trusting environment and lead to conversations about how students and teachers might support each other when setbacks occur in UxD learning experiences.

Indeed, although we tend to think that we must first build a trusting environment prior to taking risks together, the truth is by first taking risks together and having a plan of supporting each other when setbacks occur is what builds trust. Put simply: taking risks together builds collective trust[28] and, in turn, is generative of subsequent risk-taking in UxD learning experiences.

Monitoring Students' Agentic Beliefs and Self-Regulation Strategies

Finally, in addition to establishing UxD agreements and preparing students for setbacks through favorite failure narratives, another key social support is for teachers to help students monitor their beliefs and develop self-regulatory strategies. Although UxD learning experiences are designed to structure uncertainty and not overwhelm students, educators and students should still actively monitor and support agentic beliefs throughout the process.

If teachers discover that students lack confidence, fail to see the value in the project, or lack the willingness to take risks, then they can make needed adjustments. These adjustments can include everything from clarifying the task, helping students know when and how they can ask for assistance, providing students opportunities to work with peers and external support, and when it might be beneficial to add more (or less) structure to the task.

The point here is to recognize that agentic beliefs are dynamic and therefore they need to be monitored throughout the process. Agentic beliefs are also emotionally laden, so it is important to recognize and

---

[28] Grant & Coyle, "The process of building trust works in the opposite way that you think it does."

support any negative emotions that students experience when they encounter situations whereby their efforts fall short.

As has been discussed, students may believe they are capable of doing something that they value only to find out that they do not yet have the skills or knowledge to be successful. This can elicit a wide range of negative emotions and teachers should anticipate and be willing to allow students to experience these emotions,[29] but do so in a way that does not result in harmful or destructive behavior. In other words, a key aim of monitoring agentic beliefs is to help students develop self-regulatory skills when engaging in UxD learning experiences.

Researchers[30] have described how taking creative action in the face of uncertainty requires a combination of healthy agency beliefs *and* strategies to regulate their emotions. These strategies[31] include:

- *Forethought strategies.* Students can employ these strategies before engaging in a UxD task. Educators can help support students' forethought strategies by having them anticipate the uncertainties they will encounter and prepare them for exploring possibilities, seeking out multiple perspectives, asking help when they feel confused or frustrated, and getting support in deciding whether to persist with a particular approach or pursue more promising possibilities.[32]
- *Performance strategies.* Students use these strategies in the midst of UxD learning experiences. Teachers can help students learn when they might need to adjust their approach and how to regulate their emotions when encountering obstacles throughout the process. This goes beyond simply telling students, "Don't be upset" as this can be experienced as controlling rather that supportive of their autonomy.[33] Instead, teachers can acknowledge negative emotions (e.g., "I can understand why you're upset. You put a lot of work into this and it's not working out") and provide support to work through those emotions in a more productive way (e.g., "Let's take a break from this and explore some additional possibilities how you might work through this …").

---

[29] Reeve, "Why teachers adopt a controlling motivating style toward students and how they can become more autonomy supportive."
[30] Hoffmann et al., "Beyond tolerating ambiguity: How emotionally intelligent people can channel uncertainty into creativity."
[31] Zielińska & Karwowski, "Living with uncertainty in the creative process: A self-regulatory perspective."
[32] Ivcevic & Nusbaum, "From having an idea to doing something with it: Self-regulation for creativity."
[33] Reeve, "Why teachers adopt a controlling motivating style toward students and how they can become more autonomy supportive."

- *Self-reflection strategies.* Finally, students can use self-reflection strategies after they have worked through various critical moments of UxD experiences and at the end of UxD projects. Educators can support the development of these strategies by having students reflect on, share, and discuss their experiences. This includes having students discuss what went well during the experience, what didn't work, what kinds of emotions they experienced during the process, what kinds of helpful feedback and assistance they received from others, and ultimately what they learned from the process.

Summary and Next Steps

Taken together, when teachers and students actively monitor agentic beliefs in conjunction with developing strategies to help students regulate emotions, then students will be in a better position to navigate the unknown and to bring about more promising possibilities for their learning, lives, and futures. Application 7 provides several easy ways to quickly check-in with students and monitor their agentic self-beliefs throughout UxD learning experiences.

Regardless of the outcome of students' efforts, they can come to realize that going through the process, including the struggles, setbacks, and failures they face along the way, can still be beneficial for their learning and growth in the long run.[34] Part of this process includes helping students focus their efforts on trying to make a positive contribution to others, which reflects the transformative ethos of the UxD approach and is the focus of the next chapter.

---

[34] Beghetto & McBain, *My Favorite Failure*; Kapur, "Examining productive failure, productive success, unproductive failure, and unproductive success in learning."

APPLICATION 7 MONITORING AND SUPPORTING STUDENTS' AGENTIC BELIEFS

Overview

This application provides a series of monitoring and supportive prompts to help students engage with UxD learning tasks (pre-checks), sustain effort (check-ins), and reflect on their efforts (post-checks). The application also provides a brief, running narrative[35] after each set of prompts to illustrate how self-beliefs and supportive prompts might vary for students before, during, and after engaging in a UxD learning experience.

The "pre-check" prompts provide examples of quick-checks to help monitor confidence, perceived value, and risk-taking beliefs before students embark on a UxD learning experience. The supportive prompts provide examples of "just-in-time" supports that can help students seek the assistance they need to bolster their confidence, interest, and willingness to engage. These supports also offer students alternatives for adjusting the project to make it more interesting and relevant to them.

The "checking-in" prompts provide quick-checks of student self-beliefs as well as supportive prompts that can help students develop and sustain their confidence, interest, and willingness to persist (or make needed changes). Finally, the "post-check" prompts provide ways of quickly checking how the experience influenced students' self-beliefs about future projects. This includes "reflective prompts" regarding what they learned from the project, including why it is worth the effort to take the risk of engaging in UxD projects.

Application 7.1 UxD Pre-checks and Initial Supports

Self-Beliefs	Example Pre-checks	Example Initial Supports
Confidence	*Can you do this?* How confident do you feel about your ability to complete this task? Individual, written check-in: - Rate your confidence on Scale 0–10	*How can we help you prepare to do this?* - What kinds of questions do you have that would help you be more confident?

---

[35] The running narrative was developed by the author in collaboration with OpenAI's Playground GPT model.

(cont.)

Self-Beliefs	Example Pre-checks	Example Initial Supports
	(0 = Not at all confident, 10 = Extremely confident) Whole or small group check-in: - Thumbs up (Confident), Thumb sideways (Somewhat Confident); Thumbs down (Not confident).	- How can we help you now? - How can you get help along the way?
Perceived value	*Why Should you do this?* How interested are you in doing this? Individual, written check-in: - Rate Your interest on Scale 0–10 (0 = Not at all interested, 10 = Extremely interested) Whole or small group check-in: - Thumbs up (Interested), Thumb sideways (Somewhat interested); Thumbs down (Not interested). Do you see the importance in doing this? - Individual, written check-in: Rate the importance on Scale 0–10 (0 = Not at all important, 10 = Extremely important) Whole or small group check-in: - Thumbs up (Important), Thumb sideways (Somewhat important); Thumbs down (Not important).	*How can we help make this more interesting and important for you?* - What would make this more interesting or important for you? - Is there something you can add to this that would make it more interesting or important for you? - Is there a different or related project or problem you think would be more interesting or important?
Risk-taking	*Will you do this?* Are you willing to try this out? Individual, written check-in: - Rate Your willingness to try on Scale 0–10 (0 = Not at all willing to try, 10 = Extremely willing to try) Whole or small group check-in: - Thumbs up (Willing to try), Thumb sideways (Somewhat willing to try); Thumbs down (Not willing to try).	*How can we help try this?* - Is there something about this project that worries you or you have concerns about? - What might prevent you from trying? - Is there something we can help with that would enable you to be more willing to try this out? - What kinds of things can we change to help increase your willingness to try?

Running Example: Initial UxD Project Engagement

Imagine a group of middle-school students who came up with the idea of starting a project called, "Green Guardians." The project involves the members of the club engaged in activities such as planting trees, removing invasive species from natural areas, building birdhouses or bat houses for wildlife habitat restoration projects, creating trails for hikers and cyclists, and conducting stream cleanups. Initially, when the students were presented with the idea of starting the Green Guardians club they lacked confidence in facing what seemed like a daunting task. They didn't believe that their efforts would make much of a difference and lacked enthusiasm for taking on such a responsibility.

The teachers supported them through this process by breaking down each step into manageable chunks – from planning activities to finding experts who could help teach about environmental changes – so it was easier to understand how everything fits together. Through conversations, research tasks, hands-on experiences outside school grounds, or virtual field trips online via video conferencing tools, the students' teacher helped cultivate interest in exploring further just what kind of positive impact can be made.

Other members within the project offered additional support as well: older/experienced students gave advice based off their own experiences; parents provided insight into local resources available; community leaders came forward offering volunteering opportunities which allowed everyone involved (including those initially uncertain) to see firsthand why participating had its benefits both in the short term and long term.

After feeling more empowered thanks to all these sources coming together, soon enough even those lacking willingness began engaging enthusiastically with every new challenge thrown at them while working toward making lasting change happen within their community.

Application 7.2   UxD Check-ins and Timely Supports

Self-Beliefs	Example Quick-Checks	Example Timely Supports
Confidence	*How are you doing with this?* How confident are you feeling about your ability to complete this task? Individual, written check-in:	*How can we help you do this?* - What kinds of questions do you have that would help you be more confident?

(cont.)

Self-Beliefs	Example Quick-Checks	Example Timely Supports
	- Rate your confidence on Scale 0–10 *(0 = Not at all confident, 10 = Extremely confident)* Whole or small group check-in: - Thumbs up (Confident), Thumb sideways (Somewhat Confident); Thumbs down (Not confident).	- How can we help you now? - How can you get help along the way?
Perceived value	*Why Should you continue doing this?* How interested are you in continuing to do this? Individual, written check-in: - Rate Your interest on Scale 0–10 *(0 = Not at all interested, 10 = Extremely interested)* Whole or small group check-in: - Thumbs up (Interested), Thumb sideways (Somewhat interested); Thumbs down (Not interested). Do you see the importance in continuing to do this? - Individual, written check-in: Rate the importance on Scale 0–10 *(0 = Not at all important, 10 = Extremely important)* Whole or small group check-in: - Thumbs up (Important), Thumb sideways (Somewhat important); Thumbs down (Not important).	*How can we help make this more interesting and important for you?* - What would make this more interesting or important for you? - Is there something you can add to or remove from this that would make it more interesting or important for you? - Is there a different way of continuing to work on this project or problem that would make it more interesting or important to you?
Risk-taking	*Will I continue to try to do this?* Are you willing to continue trying? Individual, written check-in: - Rate Your willingness to continue trying on Scale 0–10 *(0 = Not at all willing to try, 10 = Extremely willing to try)* Whole or small group check-in: - Thumbs up (Willing to try), Thumb sideways (Somewhat willing to try); Thumbs down (Not willing to try).	*How can we help you continue?* - Is there something that is worrying you about continuing? - What do you have concerns about that is preventing you from trying? - Is there something we can help with that would enable you to continue? - What kinds of things can we change to help you continue?

Running Example: During UxD Project Engagement

As the Green Guardians project progressed, some of the students involved were overwhelmed with setbacks that they encountered. They began questioning if their efforts were really making a difference and whether this was an endeavor worth continuing. Doubts caused them to lose confidence in themselves and the value associated with such work.

The teachers provided support by facilitating conversations with each student about what it meant for them personally to be part of something greater than just individual accomplishments; reassuring everyone that no matter how small one's contribution may seem at first glance, all contributions are necessary when working toward affecting change within any given community.

Additionally, these educators also offered guidance through critiques and advice after seeing initial attempts while encouraging further exploration into different methods until success was achieved. Through patience and dedication from both sides of the partnership, progress was made – even during times when students felt a lack of motivation. By providing multiple perspectives and support, students were willing to tackle the obstacles they faced.

Application 7.3   UxD Post-checks and Reflective Supports

Self-Beliefs	Example Post-checks	Example Reflective Supports
Confidence	Can you do something similar in the future? How confident are you about being able to do projects like this in the future? Individual, written check-in: - Rate your confidence on Scale 0–10 *(0 = Not at all confident, 10 = Extremely confident)* Whole or small group check-in: - Thumbs up (Confident), Thumb sideways (Somewhat Confident); Thumbs down (Not confident).	*What did you learn from this experience?* - How did this project go for you? - What was difficult about this project? - What was most helpful to you when you felt stuck or frustrated during this project? - What would have been more helpful? - What did you learn about yourself as a result of participating in this project?

(cont.)

Self-Beliefs	Example Post-checks	Example Reflective Supports
Perceived value	Why should you do projects like this in the future? How interested are you in doing other projects like this? Individual, written check-in: - Rate Your interest on Scale 0–10 *(0 = Not at all interested, 10 = Extremely interested)* Whole or small group check-in: - Thumbs up (Interested), Thumb sideways (Somewhat interested); Thumbs down (Not interested). Do you see the importance in doing projects like this in the future? - Individual, written check-in: Rate the importance on Scale 0–10 *(0 = Not at all important, 10 = Extremely important)* Whole or small group check-in: - Thumbs up (Important), Thumb sideways (Somewhat important); Thumbs down (Not important).	Why are projects like this worth the effort? - What is the most important and interesting aspects of this project? - What would have made this project more interesting or important to you? - Who is this project benefiting? - Do you think that it is important that this project continues even after you move on? - If so, how can we ensure that this project continues? - If not, why not?
Risk-taking	Will you try to do projects like this in the future? Are you willing to try to develop a new project like this? Individual, written check-in: - Rate Your willingness to try in the future. Scale 0–10 *(0 = Not at all willing to try, 10 = Extremely willing to try)* Whole or small group check-in: - Thumbs up (Willing to try), Thumb sideways (Somewhat willing to try); Thumbs down (Not willing to try).	Why is it important to try to create and complete projects like this? - Why is it important to try to do a project like this even if you're not sure it will work out? - How did you benefit from this project? - How is this project benefiting others? - What were some of the key challenges you faced? - What did you learn from those challenges? - Do you think such projects are worth the risk of facing challenges, setbacks, and potential failures? Explain your response.

Running Example: Following UxD Project Engagement

At the end of their journey, each member of the Green Guardians project presented what they had learned about themselves and how it could be applied to future endeavors. One student shared that due to facing challenges with support and a renewed sense of perseverance, what initially felt like an insurmountable obstacle was eventually surmounted. Another student discussed having gained newfound respect for nature after seeing firsthand just how much work goes into keeping its beauty alive, whereas another student talked about how important collective action is when trying to make a positive change.

Overall, these students were proud not only because of tangible accomplishments achieved in "Green Guardian" activities, but also because they recognized the personal growth they experienced throughout the process. Many students also talked about their interest and intentions going forward – taking everything learned from this experience along with them – wherever life's path led next. They were also proud of what they contributed and looked forward to designing similar projects in the near future.

In order to make sure that the Green Guardians project continues to make a contribution once they go on to high school, these students decided it was important for them to instill enthusiasm within those who may take over stewardship of this project. To do so, the students organized outreach events which allowed younger children and other teenagers to learn more about environmental conservation as well as potential service opportunities available through joining the Green Guardian club.

Finally, outside experts (including many who originally spoke to them at the beginning of the project) were brought back in to assist in transitioning current members out and bringing new participants in. This helped to establish continuity between cohorts and enabled the project to continue on into the future.

CHAPTER 8

Making Principled Contributions

> The idea is to try to give *all* the information to help others to judge the value of your contribution; not just the information that leads to judgment in one particular direction or another.
>
> —Richard Feynman[1]
>
> It has been called the "interocular traumatic test," you know what the data mean when the conclusion hits you between the eyes.
>
> —Edwards et al., 1963, p. 217[2]
>
> I beseech ye ... think that ye may be mistaken.
>
> —Oliver Cromwell, 1650[3]

School is all about student learning. And in the prototypical, backward design arrangement we tend to judge student learning based on whether students have met specific criteria on assignments and assessments in expected ways. School-based judgments of learning take it one step further by attempting to score the percentage of criteria attained (0–100 percent) and then converting those percentages to gradations (A–F). These grades can then be averaged over time to calculate grade point averages. However, this is where judgments of school-based learning typically stop. Whether students can apply their knowledge to benefit others typically falls outside the scope of school-based assessments and grades.

Relying on grades to determine whether students have learned can lead to the absurd situation where students themselves do not know if they have "learned the material" until they receive their grades on an assignment or exam. Indeed, grades often do not reflect other important aspects of student learning and growth, such as a newfound interest in the topic,

---

[1] Feynman, "Cargo cult science."
[2] Edwards et al., "Bayesian statistical inference for psychological research."
[3] Cromwell quote from Lord et al., "Considering the opposite: A corrective strategy for social judgment."

increased confidence, or various other aspects of learning that were not adequately captured in the assessments and reflected in the grades.[4]

Uncertainty x Design (UxD) learning experiences can, of course, be squeezed into this typical assessment scheme and reified into scores and grades. But that is not the point. Rather, these kinds of experiences have the aim of providing students with an opportunity to put their learning to creative work and, ultimately, make a positive and lasting contribution to others. Moreover, UxD experiences align with the idea of providing all the information on the value of students' contribution, not just the information that leads to scores and grades. If scores and grades are not the point, then how can we know that students have learned from UxD experiences?

One way we know students have learned as a result of UxD learning experiences is because they have passed the "interocular traumatic test." That is to say, we know students have been successful in UxD experiences because the result of their efforts "hits us right between the eyes." Such contributions stand on their own and result in something beneficial that was not there before, such as a new mobile app to help local charities and nonprofits raise funds, the creation of a new community service club at their school, the development of a watershed project that protects an endangered shrimp in their state, the establishment of a daycare service for parents in their city, or the construction of a new skate park in a rural farming community.

The value of UxD learning experiences, however, is not limited to whether students create something tangible. Indeed, the process also has value in itself. Consequently, even when students' efforts do not work out or do not result in the physical or tangible creation of something new, they can still make an important contribution to themselves and others by reflecting on and sharing the stories behind their process, what they attempted to do, what worked and didn't work, and what they learned along the way.

It is in this way that UxD learning experiences are creative learning experiences in the fullest sense of the term. This is because UxD projects and activities can result in the creation of something new, beneficial, and lasting whether it be new levels of confidence and self-knowledge to development of a new, tangible product. This final chapter describes how UxD learning can be thought of as a form of creative learning and how the result of UxD learning experiences can make a positive and lasting contribution in and beyond the walls of the classroom.

[4] Zhao, "What works may hurt: Side effects in education."

UxD Learning Is Creative Learning

When we act on uncertainty and resolve it in some new and meaningful way, we have engaged in creative learning. Creative learning refers to a personal and social process that leads to new and personally meaningful insights, ideas, and actions.[5] And, as will be discussed, when students engage in the full cycle of UxD learning they can creatively contribute to the learning and lives of others.

Creative learning is not something that only certain people have the capacity to do. Rather, it is a survival imperative. Creative learning is considered an innate capacity that humans have had from the beginning of our time on this planet. It is not something that needs to be taught, like reading, writing, or computation. Rather, students already and always have the capacity to think and act in new ways under states of uncertainty, they just need opportunities to exercise and further develop that capacity.

This chapter focuses on how UxD learning experiences represent opportunities for creative learning and can thereby contribute to students' own and other's learning and life. More specifically, this chapter aims to bring together various ideas and themes presented throughout the book. Consequently, we'll need to call back upon several of those ideas and themes presented in previous chapters, not to simply repeat them but to situate them in a broader and more integrated presentation of how these ideas play out in support of students making a principled contribution to their own and others learning and lives.

Revisiting Key Features of the UxD Learning Process

Whenever students encounter uncertainty in UxD learning experiences, it can propel them into a state of creative sensemaking,[6] which enables them to not only resolve the uncertainty that they encounter but also develop new and meaningful insights and actions that can benefit others. More specifically, the uncertainty of the to-be-determined UxD elements disrupts students' routine or habitual states of knowing and doing.

Although the uncertainty that students encounter should be structured by social support (so it is not too overwhelming), it should also be sufficiently disruptive whereby neither students nor teachers know, in

---

[5] Beghetto, "Creative learning in education."
[6] Anderson et al., "Grasping the uncertainty of scientific phenomena: A creative, agentic, and multimodal model for sensemaking."

advance, how it will be resolved. Consequently, students will need to engage in *creative sensemaking*, which involves generating new possibilities for thought and action, in order to resolve the to-be-determined elements they face.

Creative sensemaking does not occur in a knowledge or experiential vacuum.[7] Rather, it occurs in the midst of students' prior experiences, knowledge, and understanding of the situation at hand and in collaboration with teachers and skilled others. Indeed, as the Pragmatic philosopher Douglas Anderson has explained, "creativity of any kind cannot begin without a certain amount of funded experience."[8]

Creative sensemaking therefore starts from somewhere and that somewhere includes curiosities, hunches, speculations, and conjectures about the ill-defined situations that students face. Importantly, these are not simply blind guesses, rather they are initial starting points whereby students explore possibilities. This exploration is, in part, supported by students' own prior knowledge and experiences and through collaboration and guidance from peers and skilled others. These collaborations help students maintain openness to new possibilities, seek out new perspectives on the UxD projects they are working on, and identify new possibilities for how they might take action to resolve the uncertainty they are experiencing.

Once possibilities have been generated, the next step of UxD learning is to select and pre-test possibilities. As has been discussed, taking creative action is how students test the viability of possibilities. Even though students may believe a possibility they generated will resolve the uncertainty they face, students will not really know unless they actually test it out. An initial, low-cost "pre-testing" step of creative learning simply involves sharing their ideas with others. This is a way for students to learn how to clearly communicate their ideas and get feedback on these ideas from others. Although this is somewhat low cost in that students are simply sharing their ideas with others prior to implementing them, it still comes with the risk of being dismissed by others.

Consequently, selecting actionable possibilities, which includes seeking feedback from others, requires students to have confidence in their own ideas, see the value in their work, and the willingness to take the risk of sharing these ideas with others. Even though seeking feedback does come with its risks, it is an important (and often necessary) step in pre-testing possibilities. It can reveal how an idea that might seem clear to the student

---

[7] Guilford, "Creativity."   [8] Anderson, *Creativity and the Philosophy of CS Peirce*.

is not clearly understood by others. This, in turn, can prompt students to rethink how to better communicate or demonstrate those ideas. Students can also be made aware of other aspects of their ideas that need additional work and effort.

Ultimately, however, students will need to act on their ideas to determine whether the possibilities they have generated will resolve the uncertainty they face. If their ideas and actions do not work out, then they will need to revise their approach or return to generating new possibilities. This process can require multiple iterations and, at each step along the way, students will need to determine whether to persist with the same possibility or pivot to a new one. The decision to persist versus pivot is not a clear-cut decision, because it can vary depending on the situation and people involved.

The good news is that there are often multiple ways to creatively resolve ill-defined problems such that the same problem may be eventually resolved either through persistence and refinement or through pivoting and trying different possibilities.[9] Teachers and external community partners can play a key role in helping students navigate this process and determine when it might be beneficial to persist or pivot during UxD learning experiences.

Regardless of the approach taken and whether students have (or have not) successfully resolved the uncertainty they have faced they can still benefit from new learnings and insights about their efforts. And if students have an opportunity to share their efforts and creations with others, including the stories behind their efforts (e.g., setbacks, pivot points, support received, and what they learned from the process), then they have a chance to contribute to others.

UxD Contributions to Oneself and Others

Although it is true that students can personally benefit from UxD learning experiences it is also true that for them to realize the full promise of the UxD approach they need to orient their efforts toward contributing to others. Educators play a key role in this process by helping students strike a balance between their own personal aspirations and interest and the interests of others.

Doing so can have the doubly mutual benefit of developing students' ability to navigate uncertainties while at the same time cultivating an ethos

---

[9] Sawyer, *Zig Zag: The Surprising Path to Greater Creativity*.

of trying to contribute to others.[10] Figure 8.1 provides a "cone of contributions" that depicts the various audiences and levels of impact students can consider when trying to make a creative contribution.

As depicted in Figure 8.1, there are at least four potential levels of impact that students can make when engaging in UxD learning experiences. Those four levels include an impact on oneself, immediate others, the broader community, and unknown and future others. Each of the four levels of impact differs by audience, context, and scope. Each will be discussed in turn.

Contributions to Oneself

Anytime students engage with uncertainty and find new and personally meaningful ways of resolving it; they make a potentially lasting impact on themselves. This can take the form of new and meaningful changes in students' thinking, behaviors, and agentic self-beliefs. In this way, the audience and context for self-contributions is the individual student (this is denoted by the shading in Figure 8.1). And the outcomes of UxD learning experiences need not rely on an external audience to make a judgment about the meaningfulness of a contribution at the personal level. This assertion aligns with the concept of "mini-c" creativity,[11] which recognizes new and personally meaningful insights and actions as creative.

Self-changes can also result when students have not fully or successfully resolved the uncertainty of a UxD learning activity or project. Indeed, as discussed in Chapter 7, even setbacks can lead to new and meaningful perspectives, insights, and behaviors. Students' personal impacts are not, of course, limited to UxD learning experiences. They also occur when students engage in most any form of learning, including the prototypical school-based learning in backward design. However, in the prototypical transactional approach of school, self-impact is where the focus often ends. In the UxD approach this is where the real work begins.

Students likely will need help developing an ethos of self-monitoring to ensure that their efforts are not only benefiting themselves, but also benefiting others. Educators play a key role here by providing structured and frequent opportunities for students to actively consider and reflect on their commitment to benefiting others. In the context of UxD learning,

---

[10] Sternberg & Chowkase, "When we teach for positive creativity, what exactly do we teach for?"
[11] Beghetto & Kaufman, "Toward a broader conception of creativity: A case for 'mini-c' creativity."

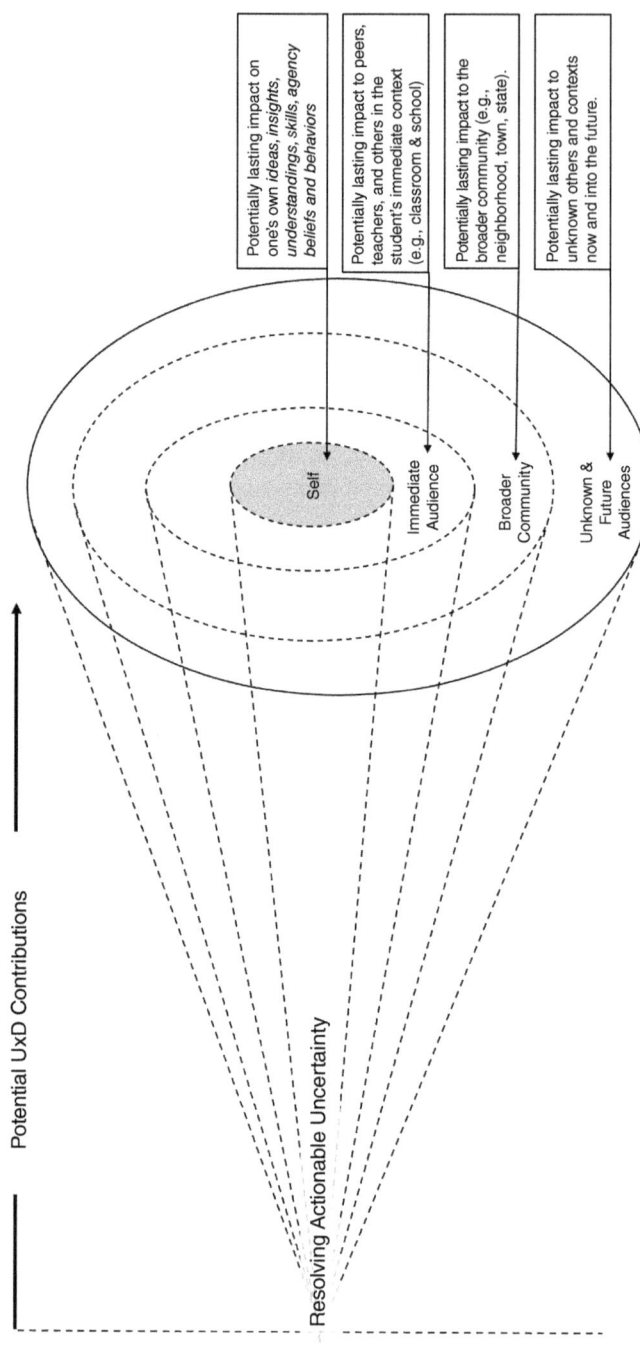

Figure 8.1 Cone of contributions

educators can use strategies presented in Applications 6 and 7 to monitor student self-beliefs and proactively consider negative outcomes.

In addition to these strategies, educators can also help students in thinking about how they can share their own learning and insights to benefit others using prompts, such as:

- *Am I willing to share what I learned to potentially benefit others' learning?*
- *If I have a good idea that might help another student or team, am I willing to share those ideas with them?*
- *Am I willing to "disagree with myself" and change my mind when I hear that what I thought was a good idea that could help others is not beneficial for a particular situation, person, group, or context?*
- *Am I willing to continue to check-in with others and make any necessary changes to my ideas, efforts, and actions to ensure that what I am doing is actually benefiting others?*

In sum, although UxD learning experiences have a goal of having a positive impact on individual students they are also guided by the transformative aim of encouraging students to go beyond the self and contribute to others in their immediate context and beyond.

Contributions to Immediate Audiences

Contributions to immediate audiences refer to contributions students can make to their peers, teachers, and other people in their immediate context. This can occur at any phase of the UxD process. A teacher could, for instance, guide students in generating possibilities for another group of students interested in coming up with a project that blends the arts with technology to represent a modern version of a historical event. Although this might occur at the early stages of a UxD project, it can still result in students making a positive impact on the project of another group of students.

Much like self-contributions, contributions to immediate others can result from engaging with most any type of UxD learning experience, but typically result from students engaging with UxD projects and learning experiences that are more localized in students' schools and classrooms.

Traditional schooling experiences provide opportunities for students to present and share their work to peers in their classroom and the broader school community. However, the main difference between traditional forms of "sharing" and UxD contributions is that UxD contributions prioritize benefiting others, while also fostering individual learning in the process.

In typical school-based sharing, the focus is on demonstrating and verifying individual students' personal understanding, with any benefits to others being secondary. Conversely, in UxD learning, contributions to others is intentional rather than incidental. Given this intentional focus, it is important for students to learn simple strategies for monitoring the impact of their UxD contributions on peers, teachers, and other members of their immediate environment.

The immediate classroom and school context provides an ideal setting for students to learn and practice strategies for monitoring immediate impact. In the classroom, students can use simple check-ins and requests for feedback from their peers and teachers, such as:

- *What did you find most helpful?*
- *What about it was helpful?*
- *How could it be more helpful?*
- *Is there something I'm/we're missing?* and
- *Is there something I/we can do now to be more helpful?*

As students' UxD work moves beyond their classrooms and into their school community, students can learn how to develop and use more systematic and formal monitoring strategies; these can include simple online surveys or brief interviews with participants and recipients of a UxD project (e.g., "Let's schedule check-ins with students in the AI club to make sure they like it and how we might improve it."). Application 8 provides an example of the kinds of questions students can ask themselves and others to monitor the impact of their school-based efforts.

Regardless of the monitoring approach students take, the key is for students to recognize and commit to the responsibility of ensuring their efforts are making a positive impact. Doing so takes on continued importance as their contributions reach beyond the walls of their schools and classrooms.

Impact to Broader Community

Although making school and classroom contributions have immediate relevance to students, the UxD approach encourages students and teachers to move beyond the walls of the classroom and consider how they might make a positive impact on the broader community. Indeed, when students and teachers reach out to the broader community, they can find community partners to support them in identifying and tackling problems that people in their community face, including problems that have yet to be defined.

There are multiple ways that students can make an impact on the broader community. One way would be to "scale out" an existing school-based UxD project. If a group of students, for instance, developed a school club that successfully addresses a need or issue in their school, they can then explore the possibility of scaling it out by contacting other schools in (or beyond) their own school district and offer to describe and help launch a similar effort in other schools.

Doing so requires being able to tell the story of the project in a concise and compelling way. This can be supported through digital technology[12] (e.g., a brief, student-directed documentary on the project) that can be posted on their school website and social media and through in-person presentations. Another way students can make an impact to the broader community is to identify a yet-to-be addressed need in their local community, which requires them to think beyond themselves, (e.g., "what is something people in our community are facing that hasn't been addressed?"). This approach puts a new twist on service learning.[13]

Service learning typically focuses on known problems that have known solutions and invites students to participate with organizations to help others. UxD community-based projects take a slightly different approach, because UxD projects are based on student-identified problems and student-identified solutions. It is in this way that community based UxD projects represent a departure from the known-knowns of community service and instead aim to have students identify and address to-be-determined problems that can make a positive impact on the broader community.

Uncertainty x Design projects therefore represent a more collaborative effort whereby students work *with* and *for* communities by identifying challenges and needs that they can help to identify, define, and address. Regardless of whether the effort to make a positive impact is made through scaling out an existing UxD effort or through the creation of a new UxD project, students will again have a shared responsibility for monitoring and evaluating the impact of their work in collaboration with the partners and participants in the broader community.

---

[12] Henriksen et al., "Infusing creativity and technology in 21st century education: A systemic view for change."
[13] Felten & Clayton, "Service-learning."

Once students identify a way that they can contribute to the broader community, they can then be prompted to consider how they can make sure that their efforts are, in fact, making a positive and lasting contribution. Again, there are several simple prompts that can guide this process, including:

- *How can we make sure that people actually want and need our help?*
- *How can we find out (e.g., maybe we need to conduct a needs assessment)?*
- *Who can help us make sure that what we are doing is valued by the people we are wanting to help?*
- *How can we periodically check-in with people to make sure that what we are doing is working and helping?*
- *What will we do if we find out that what we thought was helping isn't working?*
- *How can we make sure that our work continues to make an impact? How can we identify and make changes? Who can help us?*
- *Who can carry this work forward if we are no longer able to do so?*
- *Who can we get involved with now to help us make sure that our work has a lasting impact?*

Contributions to Unknown and Future Audiences

Finally, in addition to making an impact on known audiences, UxD learning experiences can also help young people consider and plan for making an impact on future audiences and across yet-to-be known contexts. One way to do this is to curate projects (including the stories of the process of developing those projects) and sharing those in the form of video and digital artifacts.

Indeed, digital technologies enable people to easily create, store, and share digital artifacts that can be accessed by and contribute to future, unknown audiences.[14] Doing so can help ensure that students' UxD projects and the products from these projects can be preserved and made available across time and contexts. How might this look? Let's consider an example from a case study[15] that describes how student work can, somewhat serendipitously, make an expanding and continuous contribution to future audiences shared beyond the walls of the classroom.

---

[14] Henriksen et al., "Infusing creativity and technology in 21st century education: A systemic view for change."

[15] Basu & Beghetto, "Technology as social-material mediator: From primary to secondary creativity and beyond."

A group of middle school students in India learned about a vivid and colorful art form that originated in Central India, called Gond painting, from a group of traditional artists. The students then produced their own works (impact to self) and left their artwork to dry near the classroom. This is where a teacher, Marina Basu, encountered the students' Gond paintings (impact to others in the immediate environment), which prompted creative sensemaking in Marina as she wondered whether she could develop a narrative out of some of the paintings.

Marina transformed pictures of several paintings into imagery for two narrative books. Given that Marina digitized the books, she was able to draw on them several years later, as a doctoral student, to serve as the basis for an academic article, which has since been published and can in turn contribute to future, unknown audiences.

This is an example of how student work was "picked up" by others from a chance encounter of that work in the immediate school environment and carried forward several years later into contributions to future audiences. This example also illustrates how students' work can sometimes make unexpected and extended contributions that go well beyond the immediate temporal and social context and, in turn, make future contributions to unknown audiences.

Although the probability of making a contribution to unknown, future audiences is lower than making an immediate or community-based impact, it is still possible. Consequently, students can and should be supported in considering this possibility for their projects. The following questions can orient them to this possibility and the implications of making future impacts from their work:

- *What if our work is picked up by others and makes an impact on people we don't even know?*
- *How can we trace the impact of our work into the future? Why is it important to do so?*
- *What kinds of responsibilities do we have to unknown audiences to ensure that our work is accurate, meaningful, and makes a positive impact?*
- *What does it mean that something we make in the here and now can continue on into unknown, possible futures?*
- *What do we owe to these potential future audiences?*

UxD Contributions Are Principled Contributions

Finally, given that UxD projects have an aim of contributing to others, it is important for teachers to help students learn how to take a principled approach[16] to their work. A principled approach, in the context of UxD, is guided by a shared commitment and responsibility among students and teachers to monitor whether the possibilities students develop and implement have contributed to the greater good.

Indeed, what may seem beneficial, meaningful, and helpful does not always result in contributions that others will experience as beneficial. Consequently, it is important that students and teachers spend some time at the outset and throughout the entire process of each UxD learning project to make sure that students have a plan for monitoring the potential impact of their efforts.

Taking a principled approach to UxD learning requires a different kind of thinking. Much like generating possibilities comes from "what if" and "as if" thinking, considering and correcting the impact of one's efforts requires "what if-not" and "if not-then" thinking. "What if-not" thinking involves imagining alternative and potential negative outcomes of implementing UxD possibilities (e.g., "What if our project actually does not help the families we want to help?"). "If not-then" thinking refers to actively planning for ways to address potential negative outcomes (e.g., "We should think about some reasons why our project may not actually help families and be ready to make necessary changes to our project to make sure it makes a positive impact").

Both forms of thought are central to taking a principled approach to UxD and can help ensure that students are sufficiently critical of possibilities they generate. Each is discussed in more detail in the following section. Prior to doing so, it is worth noting that this kind of principled thinking is not easy and does not come automatically, but rather needs to be supported and intentionally incorporated in UxD learning experiences.

Adopting this critical lens on possibilities is difficult, because when students put forth effort to generate and enact possibilities, they likely will feel some personal connection and investment in these efforts. We, of course, want students to maintain their enthusiasm for the possibilities they generate so that they are motivated to see those possibilities through.

The challenge, however, is that the same enthusiasm and zeal can result in diminishing or overlooking potential negative outcomes (recall the discussion of Innovator Bias, from Chapter 6). Perhaps one of the most tragic examples is the 1986 Space Shuttle Challenger explosion, which serves as one of the most harrowing, and likely preventable, technological

---

[16] Beghetto & Anderson, "Positive creativity is principled creativity"; MLFTC, "Principled innovation."

disasters in modern history. Given that this chapter focuses on making positive contributions, it is worth spending a bit more time considering accounts of how this disaster occurred. Not because students will be engaging in such high stake's efforts, but because it can serve as an instructive example of how even highly skilled experts and decision-makers can fail to acknowledge and address potential negative outcomes when implementing innovative projects.

On January 28, 1986, there was a catastrophic failure in the solid-state rocket boosters that resulted in the explosion of Challenger Space Shuttle and total loss of the seven-member crew aboard, which included the schoolteacher, S. Christa McAuliffe. The launch and explosion were broadcast on television and viewed by thousands, including children in school. A Presidential Commission and the Committee on Science and Technology determined that the explosion was due to a failed seal in the joint of the right solid rocket booster.

Before the launch, engineers raised concerns about the safety of moving forward with the launch because of the unusually cold weather that day and long-standing knowledge and concerns about the potential for the O-ring seals on the boosters to fail and result in a catastrophic explosion. Managers from NASA and Thiokol, the company that designed the boosters, decided to move forward with the launch despite concerns raised by engineers and knowledge of the potentially deadly flaws.

As the members of the congressional Committee on Science and Technology described in their 1986 report:

> Information on the flaws in the joint design and on the problems encountered in missions prior to 51-L was widely available and had been presented to all levels of Shuttle management. Despite the presence of significant amounts of information and the occurrence of at least one detailed briefing ... technical managers failed to understand or fully accept the seriousness of the problem ... No one suggested grounding the fleet, nor did NASA embark on a concerted effort to remedy the deficiencies in O-ring performance. Rather, NASA chose to continue to fly with a flawed design.[17]

The Challenger example serves as a stark reminder of the dangers of innovator bias, in which managers downplayed potential risks and serious concerns in favor of moving a project forward. Of course, the potential risks of UxD projects and activities come nowhere near the level of hazardous behavior demonstrated in the Challenger example. Rather, this

[17] Committee on Science and Technology, "Investigation of the challenger accident."

example (and examples like them) can help young people understand the importance of taking a principled approach to their work. And UxD projects can help students learn how to do so by anticipating and proactively addressing potential unintended consequences, even in smaller scale projects.

Indeed, UxD learning experiences can help students learn how to maintain their enthusiasm about their work while simultaneously monitoring and making necessary corrections whenever their efforts are not benefiting others. Consequently, in addition to using the generative forms of "what if" and "as if" thinking in UxD projects, a more principled approach includes "what if-not" thinking and "if not-then" thinking. Each of these two forms of thinking will be discussed in more detail below, including how they can be combined to result in more principled and positive impacts on others.

"What If-Not" Thinking

"What if-not" thinking involves considering the *opposite* of possibilities generated through "what if" and "as if" thinking. "What if-not" thinking is a modern version of Cromwells' plea to consider whether what we think is good and correct is actually mistaken. Put simply, "what if-not" thinking requires considering the opposite of what we are trying to do. Considering "the opposite" represents a long recognized, yet often overlooked, remedy for biases in social and personal judgments.

Indeed, researchers have demonstrated that using the strategy of considering the opposite when making social judgments can have a substantially more corrective effect on biased thinking as compared to instructing people to "be as fair and unbiased as possible."[18] This strategy has also been successfully used by researchers as a cure for innovator bias. As mentioned in Chapter 6, researchers have shown that innovator bias can be reduced when people actively consider potential negative outcomes of their innovations. The good news is this can be done without undermining our enthusiasm for the innovation.[19]

In the context of UxD learning, teachers can support students by helping them engage in "what if-not" thinking whenever they have generated a possibility they are excited about implementing (see also Part II of the possibility thinking protocol in Application 6). This approach helps

---

[18] Lord et al., "Considering the opposite: A corrective strategy for social judgment."
[19] Reece et al., "Enforcing pragmatic future-mindedness cures the innovator's bias."

students identify potential hazards and prepares them to develop a plan for actively monitoring the impact of their work. "What if-not" thinking doesn't end here. Rather, the next step is "if not-then" thinking, which helps students consider contingency plans for situations where their initial ideas may not produce expected results.

"If Not-Then" Thinking

Computer programmers often use conditional logic in the form of "if-then-else" statements to direct the program if certain conditions are not met. This conditional logic is used to guide the operations of computers (e.g., "*If* the user enters the correct password when prompted, *then* grant access; *else* deny access and prompt the user to enter the correct password"). This conditional has been made more intuitive for students in UxD learning by using the "if not-then" formulation.

"If not-then" thinking is a way of considering and planning for contingencies if possibilities do not turn out. The "if not" portion of this thinking refers to the various potential negative outcomes generated by "what if-not" thinking. And the "then" portion of "if not-then" thinking prompts students to come up with alternatives of what to do if things don't work out. This form of thinking enables students to anticipate challenges and commit to making changes and corrections if their efforts are not resulting in beneficial outcomes to others.

When students use "if not-then" thinking before implementing a possibility, they become better equipped to recognize the need for monitoring the impact of their efforts and have an idea of how to make "as-needed" corrections along the way. In doing so, they can develop an informal and more systematic way of monitoring whether their efforts result in positive contributions to themselves and others.

Taken together, when these types of thinking are combined students will be able to adopt a more principled approach to generating possibilities and anticipate potential outcomes of their work. This includes monitoring and proactively addressing potentially negative consequences. Figure 8.2 illustrates an example of how these types of thinking can be integrated into the UxD process to generate possibilities, anticipate potential setbacks before implementation, and identify aspects of the work that may need to be monitored to ensure that students' efforts benefit others.

The example diagrammed in Figure 8.2 represents a hypothetical UxD project led by a group of 6th graders. In the example, students identify a need in their local community that they see as having the potential of

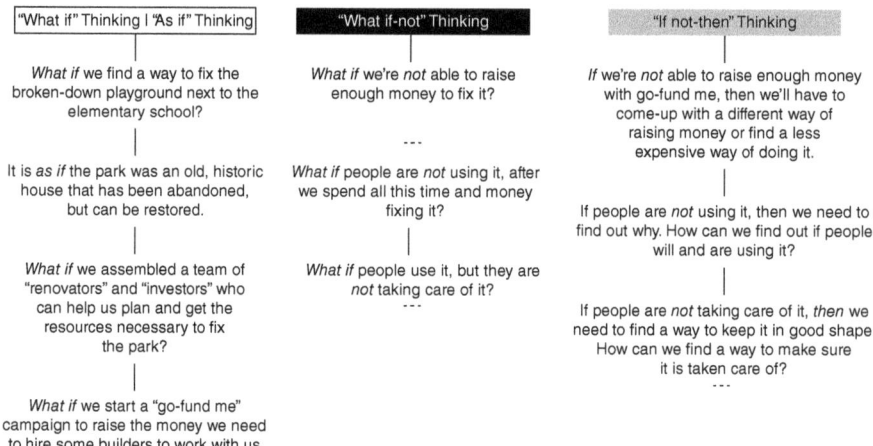

Figure 8.2   Types of generative and principled reasoning in UxD

benefiting younger students and other members of their community: renovating a run-down playground next to a local elementary school.

Through the use of "what if" and "as if" thinking, they generate ideas for how they might renovate the playground. These forms of possibility thinking can create a lot of excitement, because the possibilities are produced by students themselves. Consequently, students have increased investment and enthusiasm in trying to see these possibilities through to action. As mentioned, left unchecked, enthusiasm for ideas can have the downside of minimizing or overlooking potential hazards.

Equipped with this understanding, the 6th grade team can be supported in taking a principled approach to this project. Rather than trying to immediately implement their possibilities (e.g., start making a go-fund-me campaign), they can be encouraged to first engage in "what if-not" thinking and consider potential setbacks and challenges that they might encounter so that their work is not only successful, but actually makes a positive impact on others and their surrounding community.

Then, by combining "what if-not" thinking with "if not-then" thinking students can consider contingencies and actions they can take to ensure a more successful and positive impact of their efforts. This might include:

- developing a plan to involve additional members of their school and local community to think through various contingencies (e.g., alternative sources of funding and resources if the initial possibilities fall through),

- designing a needs-assessment strategy to understand why the playground fell into disrepair in the first place (e.g., the equipment was not well suited for elementary students and local families),
- exploring whether people would actually be interested in using the renovated park (e.g., What would elementary students and families like to see in the new play area?), and
- establishing a maintenance and sustainability plan for the playground (e.g., Who is responsible for monitoring maintenance needs, how can they partner with local members of the community to help with the maintenance of the park, and who can take over the work once they move on to high school?).

In sum, a principled approach tempers the desire to take quick action and replaces it with the development of a more comprehensive, collaborative plan for taking action and monitoring the impact of those actions.

Summary and Next Steps

UxD experiences carry the same promise and responsibility for students as they do for educators using such designs: the potential to help make an impact on possible futures. Application 8 provides templates for helping students plan UxD projects that take a more principled approach to their work by actively monitoring the contribution of their efforts.

Doing so can help students move toward a more transformative ethos of UxD. This requires an extra level of consideration, vetting, and validation to anticipate and proactively address negative unintended consequences or harmful side effects. Consequently, this increases the likelihood that their efforts result in positive benefits to their own and others' learning and lives.

APPLICATION 8 HOW CAN WE ENSURE THAT OUR WORK IS BENEFITING OTHERS?

This application provides two example templates that can be used to help students plan UxD projects and monitor the contribution of their work. It also includes two examples of what a completed template might look like for a hypothetical group of middle school students. Prompts can be added and modified for a particular context, population, and goals of the UxD project. Note: The hypothetical examples were developed and refined by the author in collaboration with OpenAI's GPT-3 models.

Application 8.1 UxD Planning and Impact Monitoring Template

Project name:	
Project team:	*We are:*
What are you planning to do?	*We want to:*
How do you plan to do it?	*We plan to do this by:*
What help do you need?	*We need help with:*
What contribution will you make?	*Self:*
	Immediate others:
	Broader community:
	Future audiences:
How will you monitor your contribution to yourself and others?	*We will make sure we are making a difference by:*
How can you make sure that this project continues?	*We will make sure this project continues by:*

Application 8.2 Example of UxD Planning and Impact Monitoring

Project name:	"Helping Kids Help Others"
Project team:	We are a group of three 8th grade students, two 7th grade students, and three 6th grade students.
What are you planning to do?	We want to start a club at our school that gets other kids involved in helping people in need (e.g., create a food pantry for hungry people in our town).

(cont.)

How do you plan to do it?	We plan to do this by talking to people in our town to find out what they need, come-up with ways to help those people, and work together to help them.
What help do you need?	We need help raising money to buy things that people need. We also need help from businesses and maybe some other adult helpers or mentors who can help us get this club started.
What contribution will you make?	*Self* – Become a better problem solver, become more confident in being a leader for this club, learn how to work with others, learn how to help others, and learn how to make our town a better place.
	Immediate others – Help other kids learn how to make a difference to our town and see why it is important to help.
	Broader community – Help people in our town who need our help.
	Future audiences – Other schools and kids can learn from our example and maybe start their own club at their school and in their town.
How will you monitor your contribution to yourself and others?	We will make sure we are making a difference by:
	- having regular check-ins with our team, teacher, and mentors
	- check-in with other kids in the club to make sure they are doing their part and learning how to help.
	- getting feedback from people we are helping.
How can you make sure that this project continues?	We will make sure this project continues by:
	- having other 6th and 7th graders get involved.
	- talking with our teachers and principal to make sure that they can help the club continue each year.
	- talking with people in our town to make sure they will continue to help the club in the future.

Application 8.3 Post-project Reflection Template

Project name:	
Project team:	*We are:*
What did you do?	*We decided to:*
What changes did you make to your initial plan?	*We initially planned to:*
Who helped you?	*We got help from:*
What contribution did you make?	*We made a difference by:*
What did you learn from this process?	*We learned:*
What would you do differently if you could do this project again?	*If we could do this again, we would:*
How will the project continue?	*Our project will continue because:*

Application 8.4 Example of Post-project Reflection

Project name:	"Helping Kids Help Others"
Project team:	We are a group of three 8th grade students, two 7th grade students, and three 6th grade students.
What did you do?	*We decided to* create a website to spread awareness of our club, get donations, and volunteers to help us plan events to help people in our town. The donations allowed us to provide clothing and other things that families in our town needed. We were able to get other kids and adults to volunteer and help us figure out who to help, collect donations, and get people what they needed.
What changes did you make to your initial plan?	We initially planned to create a food pantry, but after talking with local organizations, we realized that the best way to help those in need was to create a website to let people know about our club and they could let us know what they needed. We found out that there were a lot of families in our town that we could help.
Who helped you?	We got help from other kids at our school and adults in our town. We also received donations from anonymous donors, businesses, and

(cont.)

	organizations in our town. We also got a lot of help from our teachers, the school counselor, our families, and our friends.
What contribution did you make?	We made a difference by providing families in our town by getting them clothes and other things they needed. We also made a difference to other kids by helping them learn how they could help by working together with teachers and people in our town. We also set an example for future kids, because we told the story of our club on our website so they can learn how to create the same kind of club at their own school and make a difference in their own city or town.
What did you learn from this process?	We learned: - the importance of helping families who need assistance. - the importance of planning and being okay with changing our initial idea to help people in different ways. - how to work together to achieve a goal. - how to design a website and work with organizations in our town to figure out what people need and come-up with ways to help. - how to get other kids involved to make sure the project continues.
What would you do differently if you could do this project again?	If we did this again, we would spend more time learning about what people need in our town first, instead of guessing that they need something we think they need (like a food pantry). We would also make sure to get mentors, people, organizations, and businesses involved earlier in the planning of our club.
How will the project continue?	Our project will continue because: - we have 6th and 7th graders involved who plan to continue the project next year, - our teachers and principal said they will help keep the club going, - we also have mentors and donors that want to continue to help our club, - our website will keep the project going too, and - we also have plans for how our club can do fundraisers throughout the year at our school to help with donations.

AVANTI

From What Is to What Could Be

> The beginning is always today.
> —Attributed to Mary Wollstonecraft Shelley
>
> Possible is more a matter of attitude,
> A matter of decision, to choose
> Among the impossible possibilities,
> When one sound opportunity
> Becomes a possible solution.
> —Dejan Stojanovic[1]

This book has served as a prolonged exercise in possibility thinking, aimed at imagining new, educational futures that can better support students in learning how to navigate uncertainties and contribute to their own and others' learning and lives. As with any futures scenario, this is not the end but only the beginning. Movement from the actual to the possible requires a willingness to not only imagine new possibilities, but to choose to put those into action. The ideas, principles, and tools presented in this book offer educators, students, researchers, and all of us a starting point for developing and testing out the Uncertainty x Design (UxD) approach and working toward more promising educational futures.

With respect to educators, the UxD approach offers ideas and tools to help them support students in becoming the creative authors of their own futures. Many of the ideas and tools can (and should) be modified to fit a particular population of students and school context. Through testing, refinement, and collaboration with students and external partners, these tools provide a starting point for educators to experiment with new possibilities and determine how they can best be applied to – and push beyond – their current instructional efforts.

---

[1] This is an excerpt from the poem, "Possibility" by Dejan Stajanovic. https://archive.org/details/DejanStojanovic.

Doing so will require a change in thinking about the logic of teaching and willingness to embrace the uncertainty of the UxD approach. The good news is the UxD approach is grounded in the principle of structured uncertainty, so most educators are already at least halfway along the path to UxD. What is needed is to balance the structure and support they already provide for students with more opportunities for students to tackle the unknown.

With respect to students, the ideas and tools offered in this book provide a means for students to take charge of their own learning and put it to creative use to benefit others, their futures, and world around them. Students are ready. We just need to support them in moving forward. Parents, educators, and members of the broader community do not need to wait, they can start now by trying out the ideas presented in this book to design learning experiences for students in and outside of this place called "school."

With respect to researchers, the ideas presented in this book should be further tested and developed by additional research. However, given that the logic of the design offered by UxD is different, the logic of research on these designs should also be different. Although there is benefit in conducting research *about* UxD designs to test out whether, how, and in what situations learning based on this approach might better support students' confidence and competence in navigating current and future uncertainties, traditional research approaches are not sufficient.

Indeed, a different approach for UxD research is needed. Such an approach would complement and push beyond research *about* UxD learning experiences and include research *with* education. Research *with* education is an approach aimed at broadening the horizon of what is possible for researchers, educators, and students. Such research can showcase the scenario building processes by which the UxD approach can be designed and implemented in different contexts with different populations of students, including the challenges, insights, learnings, and opportunities that come with efforts aimed at implementing UxD learning designs.

Change is upon us. The beginning of a new approach to education is today. And the time is *now* for all of us to assume the responsibility of working toward supporting students in becoming the creative authors of their own futures. We can no longer wait for "someday" to take action. We owe students much more in their educational experiences right now.

References

AACTE + Partnership for 21st Century Skills. (2010). 21st century knowledge and skills in educator preparation. https://files.eric.ed.gov/fulltext/ED519336.pdf

Acar, S., & Runco, M. A. (2019). Divergent thinking: New methods, recent research, and extended theory. *Psychology of Aesthetics, Creativity, and the Arts, 13*(2), 153–158. https://doi.org/10.1037/aca0000231

Ahvenharju, S., Lalot, F., Minkkinen, M., & Quiamzade, A. (2021). Individual futures consciousness: Psychology behind the five-dimensional Futures Consciousness scale. *Futures, 128.* https://doi.org/10.1016/j.futures.2021.102708

Alexander, P. A., Schallert, D. L., & Reynolds, R. E. (2009). What is learning anyway? A topographical perspective considered. *Educational Psychologist, 44*(3), 176–192. https://doi.org/10.1080/00461520903029006

Ambrose, D. (2022). Discovering and dismantling enormous barriers hindering the transition from transactional to transformational giftedness. In R. J. Sternberg, D. Ambrose, & S. Karami (Eds.), *The Palgrave Handbook of Transformational Giftedness for Education* (pp. 1–21). Cham: Springer.

Anderson, D. R. (2013). *Creativity and the Philosophy of CS Peirce* (vol. 27). Dordrecht, The Netherlands: Springer Science & Business Media.

Anderson, R. C., Irvin, S., Bousselot, T., Beard, N., & Beach, P. (2022). Grasping the uncertainty of scientific phenomena: A creative, agentic, and multimodal model for sensemaking. In R. A. Beghetto & G. Jaeger (Eds.). *Uncertainty: A Catalyst for Creativity, Learning and Development* (pp. 159–179). Cham: Springer.

Appadurai, A. (2013). *The Future as Cultural Fact.* London: Verso.

Arendt, H. (1998/1958). *The Human Condition.* Chicago: The University of Chicago Press.

Argyris, C., & Schon, D. A. (1992). *Theory in Practice: Increasing Professional Effectiveness.* San Francisco: John Wiley & Sons.

Bandura, A. (1997). *Self-Efficacy: The Exercise of Control.* New York: Macmillan.

Barber, M., Analyst, S., & Vic, B. (2006). Wildcards: Signals from a future near you. *Journal of Futures Studies, 11*(1), 75–94.

Bardt, C. (2019). *Material and Mind.* Cambridge, MA: The MIT Press.

Basu, M., & Beghetto, R. A. (2021). Technology as social-material mediator: From primary to secondary creativity and beyond. *Creativity. Theories–Research–Applications*, *8*(1), 11–22.

Baumeister, R. F., Bratslavsky, E., Finkenauer, C., & Vohs, K. D. (2001). Bad is stronger than good. *Review of General Psychology*, *5*(4), 323–370.

Baumeister, R. F., Vohs, K. D., & Oettingen, G. (2016). Pragmatic prospection: How and why people think about the future. *Review of General Psychology*, *20*(1), 3–16. https://doi.org/10.1037/gpr0000060

Beghetto, R. A. (2007). Ideational code-switching: Walking the talk about supporting student creativity in the classroom. *Roeper Review*, *29*(4), 265–270.

(2007). Prospective teachers' beliefs about students' goal orientations: A carry-over effect of prior schooling experiences? *Social Psychology of Education*, *10*(2), 171–191.

(2013). Nurturing creativity in the micro-moments of the classroom. In K. H. Kim, J. C. Kaufman, J. Baer, & B. Sriraman (Eds.). *Creatively Gifted Students Are Not Like Other Gifted Students* (pp. 3 – 15). Leiden, The Netherlands: Brill.

(2017). Legacy projects: Helping young people respond productively to the challenges of a changing world. *Roeper Review*, *39*(3), 187–190. https://doi.org/10.1080/02783193.2017.1318998

(2017). Lesson unplanning: Toward transforming routine tasks into non-routine problems. *ZDM Mathematics Education*, *49*(7), 987–993. https://doi.org/10.1007/s11858-017-0885-1

(2018). Taking beautiful risks in education. *Educational Leadership*, *76*(4), 18–24.

(2018). *What If? Building students' problem-solving through complex challenges*. Alexandria, VA: ASCD.

(2019). Structured uncertainty: How creativity thrives under constraints and uncertainty. In C. A. Mullen (Ed.), *Creativity under Duress in Education? Creativity Theory and Action in Education* (vol. 3, pp. 27–40). Cham: Springer. https://doi.org/10.1007/978-3-319-90272-2_2

(2020). Uncertainty. In V. P. Glaveanu (Ed.). *The Palgrave Encyclopedia of the Possible*. Cham: Palgrave Macmillan. https://doi.org/10.1007/978-3-319-98390-5_122-1

(2021). Creative learning in education. In M. L. Kern & M. L. Wehmeyer (Eds.), *The Palgrave Handbook of Positive Education* (pp. 473–491). Cham: Palgrave Macmillan. https://doi.org/10.1007/978-3-030-64537-3.

(2021). How times of crisis serve as a catalyst for creative action: An agentic perspective. *Frontiers in Psychology*, *11*. https://doi.org/10.3389/fpsyg.2020.600685

(2021). There is no creativity without uncertainty: Dubito ergo creo. *Journal of Creativity*, *31*. https://doi.org/10.1016/j.yjoc.2021.100005

(2023). A new horizon for possibility thinking: A conceptual case study of Human × AI collaboration. *Possibility Studies & Society*. https://doi.org/10.1177/27538699231160136

(in press). Uncertainty as a lever for change and innovation. In D. D. Preiss, M. Singer, & J. C. Kaufman (Eds.). *Creativity, Innovation, and Change across Cultures*. London: Palgrave.

Beghetto, R. A., & Anderson, R. C. (2022). Positive creativity is principled creativity. *Education Sciences*, *12*(3), 184. https://doi.org/10.3390/educsci12030184

Beghetto, R. A., & Dilley, A. E. (2016). Creative aspirations or pipe dreams? Toward understanding creative mortification in children and adolescents. *New Directions for Child and Adolescent Development*, 151, 85–95.

Beghetto, R. A., & Karwowski, M. (2017). Toward untangling creative self-beliefs. In M. Karwowski & J. C. Kaufman (Eds.), *The Creative Self: Effect of Beliefs, Self-Efficacy, Mindset, and Identity* (pp. 3–22). Cambridge, MA: Academic Press.

Beghetto, R. A., Karwowski, M., & Reiter-Palmon, R. (2021). Intellectual risk taking: A moderating link between creative confidence and creative behavior? *Psychology of Aesthetics, Creativity, and the Arts*, *15*(4), 637–644. https://doi.org/10.1037/aca0000323

Beghetto, R. A., & Kaufman, J. C. (2007). Toward a broader conception of creativity: A case for "mini-c" creativity. *Psychology of Aesthetics, Creativity, and the Arts*, *1*(2), 73–79. https://doi.org/10.1037/1931-3896.1.2.73

Beghetto, R. A., & McBain, L. (2022). *My Favorite Failure*. Lanham, MD: Rowman & Littlefield.

Berg, J. M. (2019). When silver is gold: Forecasting the potential creativity of initial ideas. *Organizational Behavior and Human Decision Processes*, *154*, 96–117. https://doi.org/10.1016/j.obhdp.2019.08.004

Black, P., & Wiliam, D. (1998). Inside the black box: Raising standards through classroom assessment. *Phi Delta Kappan*, *80*, 139–148.

Bong, M., & Skaalvik, E. M. (2003). Academic self-concept and self-efficacy: How different are they really? *Educational Psychology Review*, *15*(1), 1–40. https://doi.org/10.1023/A:1021302408382

Brandon, L. E., Reis, S. M., Renzulli, J. S., & Beghetto, R. A. (2022). Examining teachers' perspectives of school-based opportunities and support for student creativity with the ICI Index. *Creativity Research Journal*. https://doi.org/10.1080/10400419.2022.2110416

Brown, S. I., & Walter, M. I. (2004). *The Art of Problem Posing* (3rd ed.). Mahwah, NJ: Lawrence Erlbaum Associates. https://doi.org/10.4324/9781410611833

Buhr, K., & Dugas, M. J. (2002). The intolerance of uncertainty scale: Psychometric properties of the English version. *Behaviour Research and Therapy*, *40*(8), 931–946. https://doi.org/10.1016/S0005-7967(01)00092-4

Butterscotch, J. (2022, September 6). Exploring the relationship between tolerance of ambiguity and critical thinking. https://doi.org/10.31219/osf.io/xnbjy

Castles, A., Rastle, K., & Nation, K. (2018). Ending the reading wars: Reading acquisition from novice to expert. *Psychological Science in the Public Interest*, *19*, 5–51. https://doi.org/10.1177/1529100618772271

Catmull, E., & Wallace, A. (2014). *Creativity, Inc.: Overcoming the Unseen Forces That Stand in the Way of True Inspiration.* New York: Random House.

Claxton, G. (2008). *What's the Point of School? Rediscovering the Heart of Education.* Oxford: Oneworld publications.

Clifford, J. S., Boufal, M. M., & Kurtz, J. E. (2004). Personality traits and critical thinking skills in college students: Empirical tests of a two-factor theory. *Assessment, 11*(2), 169–176.

Committee on Science and Technology. (1986). *Investigation of the Challenger Accident.* House of Representatives, Ninety-Ninth Congress (Second Session). Washington, DC. www.govinfo.gov/content/pkg/GPO-CRPT-99hrpt1016/pdf/GPO-CRPT-99hrpt1016.pdf

Craft, A. (2015). Possibility thinking: From what is to what might be. In Rupert Wegerif, Li Li, & James C. Kaufman (Eds.). *The Routledge International Handbook of Research on Teaching Thinking* (pp. 177–191). New York: Routledge.

Cropley, A. J. (2006). In praise of convergent thinking. *Creativity Research Journal, 18*(3), 391–404.

Csikszentmihalyi, M., & Getzels, J. W. (1971). Discovery-oriented behavior and the originality of creative products: A study with artists. *Journal of Personality and Social Psychology, 19*(1), 47–52. https://doi.org/10.1037/h0031106

Dahl, D. W., & Moreau, P. (2002). The influence and value of analogical thinking during new product ideation. *Journal of Marketing Research, 39*(1), 47–60. https://doi.org/10.1509/jmkr.39.1.47.18930

Dator, J. (2019). What futures studies is, and is not. In *J. Dator: A Noticer in Time.* Anticipation Science. Cham: Springer. https://doi.org/10.1007/978-3-030-17387-6_1van

Dewey, J. (1897). My pedagogic creed. *School Journal, 54,* 77–80.

(1897). The psychology of effort. *Philosophical Review, 6,* 43–56.

(1910). *How We Think.* Boston: D.C. Heath.

(2005). *Art as Experience.* New York: Perigee Books. (Original work published 1934.)

Drake, D. (2016). Sit with Us creator Natalie Hampton's crusade to help bullied teens feel included. Wharton Global Youth Program. https://globalyouth.wharton.upenn.edu/articles/podcasts/sit-us-creator-natalie-hamptons-crusade-help-bullied-teens-feel-included/

Eccles, J. S., & Wigfield, A. (1995). In the mind of the actor: The structure of adolescents' achievement task values and expectancy-related beliefs. *Personality and Social Psychology Bulletin, 21,* 215–225. http://doi.org/10.1177/0146167295213003

Edwards, W., Lindman, H., & Savage, L. J. (1963). Bayesian statistical inference for psychological research. *Psychological Review, 70*(3), 193–242. https://doi.org/10.1037/h0044139

Elliot, A. J., Dweck, C. S., & Yeager, D. S. (Eds.). (2017). *Handbook of Competence and Motivation: Theory and Application.* New York: Guilford Publications.

Felten, P., & Clayton, P. H. (2011). Service-learning. *New Directions for Teaching and Learning, 2011*(128), 75–84.

Festinger, L. (1957). *A Theory of Cognitive Dissonance.* Evanston, IL: Row, Peterson.
Feynman, R. (1974). Cargo cult science. *Engineering and Science, 37,* 10–13.
Freeston, M. H., Rhéaume, J., Letarte, H., Dugas, M. J., & Ladouceur, R. (1994). Why do people worry? *Personality and Individual Differences, 17* (6), 791–802.
Gaffney, H., Ttofi, M. M., & Farrington, D. P. (2021). What works in anti-bullying programs? Analysis of effective intervention components. *Journal of School Psychology, 85,* 37–56.
Gajda, A., Beghetto, R. A., & Karwowski, M. (2017). Exploring creative learning in the classroom: A multi-method approach. *Thinking Skills and Creativity, 24,* 250–267.
Gall, T., Vallet, F., & Yannou, B. (2022). How to visualise futures studies concepts: Revision of the futures cone. *Futures, 143,* 103024.
Gallop, D., Willy, C., & Bischoff, J. (2016). How to catch a black swan: Measuring the benefits of the premortem technique for risk identification. *Journal of Enterprise Transformation, 6,* 87–106.
Getzels, J. W. (1964). Creative thinking, problem solving, and instruction. In E. R. Hilgard (Ed.), *Theories of Learning and Instruction* (pp. 240–267). Chicago: University of Chicago Press.
Gibson, C., & Mumford, M. D. (2013). Evaluation, criticism, and creativity: Criticism content and effects on creative problem solving. *Psychology of Aesthetics, Creativity, and the Arts, 7*(4), 314–331. https://doi.org/10.1037/a0032616
Gibson, J. J. (1979). *The Ecological Approach to Visual Perception.* Boston: Houghton Mifflin.
Glăveanu, V. P. (2020). *The Possible: A Sociocultural Theory.* New York: Oxford University Press.
Glăveanu, V. P., & Beghetto, R. A. (2021). Creative experience: A non-standard definition of creativity. *Creativity Research Journal, 33*(2), 75–80. https://doi.org/10.1080/10400419.2020.1827606
(in preparation). *Pedagogies of the Possible.* New York: Cambridge University Press.
Glăveanu, V. P., Corazza, G. E., & Ness, I. J. (2023). Dialogical provocations: A creative trialogue. In D. Henriksen & P. Mishra (Eds.), *Creative Provocations: Speculations on the Future of Creativity, Technology & Learning* (pp. 213–227). Cham: Springer International Publishing.
Gleick, J. (2001). *Nature's Chaos.* New York: Hachette Book Group.
Godwin, K. E., Seltman, H., Almeda, M., Skerbetz, M. D., Kai, S., Baker, R. S., & Fisher, A. V. (2021). The elusive relationship between time on-task and learning: Not simply an issue of measurement. *Educational Psychology, 41*(4), 502–519. https://doi.org/10.1080/01443410.2021.1894324
Goodlad, J. L. (2004). *A Place Called School: Prospects for the Future.* New York: McGraw Hill.
Grant, A., & Coyle, D. (2018). The process of building trust works in the opposite way that you think it does. Retrieved from https://work.qz.com/

1241911/daniel-coyle-author-of-the-the-culture-code-says-building-trust-works-in-the-opposite-way-you-think-it-does/?mc_cid=015ae0d31b&mc_eid=427e2dccd0

Greene, M. (1995). *Releasing the Imagination: Essays on Education, the Arts, and Social Change.* San Francisco: Jossey-Bass.

Guilford, J. P. (1950). Creativity. *American Psychologist, 5,* 444–454.

Guo, Y., Lin, S., Acar, S., Jin, S., Xu, X., Feng, Y., & Zeng, Y. (2022). Divergent thinking and evaluative skill: A meta-analysis. *Journal of Creative Behavior, 56*(3), 432–448. https://doi.org/10.1002/jocb.539

Gustafson, K. (2010). Strategic horizons: Futures forecasting and the British Intelligence Community. *Intelligence and National Security, 25*(5), 589–610. https://doi.org/10.1080/02684527.2010.537118

Gustafsson, E. (2023). How can contextual variables influence creative thinking? Contributions from the optimal-level of arousal model. *Journal of Creative Behavior, 57*(1), 96–108. https://doi.org/10.1002/jocb.565

Hakan, T. (2022). Philosophy of science and black swan. *Child's Nervous System, 38,* 1655–1657. https://doi.org/10.1007/s00381-020-05009-3

Hannon, V., & Peterson, A. (2021). *Thrive: The Purpose of Schools in a Changing World.* New York: Cambridge University Press.

Hanson, M. (2023). Student loan debt statistics. EducationData.org. https://educationdata.org/student-loan-debt-statistics

Hausman, C. R. (1984). *A Discourse on Novelty and Creation.* Albany: State University of New York Press.

Heinrich, C. (2000). *Monet.* Cologne, Germany: Taschen.

Henriksen, D., Mishra, P., & Fisser, P. (2016). Infusing creativity and technology in 21st century education: A systemic view for change. *Journal of Educational Technology & Society, 19*(3), 27–37. www.jstor.org/stable/jeductechsoci.19.3.27

Henry Ford Foundation. (2023). A framework using the steps of the invention process. https://inhub.thehenryford.org/curriculum-resources/invention-convention-curriculum

Hoffmann, J. D., McGarry, J., & Seibyl, J. (2022). Beyond tolerating ambiguity: How emotionally intelligent people can channel uncertainty into creativity. In R. A. Beghetto & G. J. Jaeger (Eds.), *Uncertainty: A Catalyst for Creativity, Learning and Development* (pp. 59–79). Cham: Springer. https://doi.org/10.1007/978-3-030-98729-9_5

Inayatullah, S. (2013). Futures studies: Theories and methods. In F. G. Junquera (Ed.), *There's a Future: Visions for a Better World* (pp. 33–36). Madrid, Spain: BBVA.

Ivcevic, Z., & Hoffmann, J. D. (2022). The creativity dare: Attitudes toward creativity and prediction of creative behavior in school. *Journal of Creative Behavior, 56,* 239–257. https://doi.org/10.1002/jocb.527

Ivcevic, Z., & Nusbaum, E. C. (2017). From having an idea to doing something with it: Self-regulation for creativity. In M. Karwowski & J. C. Kaufman (Eds.), *The Creative Self: Effect of Beliefs, Self-Efficacy, Mindset, and Identity* (pp. 343–365). Cambridge, MA: Academic Press. https://doi.org/10.1016/B978-0-12-809790-8.00020-0

Jackson, J. J., Hill, P. L., Payne, B. R., Roberts, B. W., & Stine-Morrow, E. A. L. (2012). Can an old dog learn (and want to experience) new tricks? Cognitive training increases openness to experience in older adults. *Psychology and Aging, 27*(2), 286–292. https://doi.org/10.1037/a0025918

Jefferson, M., & Anderson, M. (2017). *Transforming Schools: Creativity, Critical Reflection, Communication, Collaboration*. London: Bloomsbury.

Kagan, J. (1972). Motives and development. *Journal of Personality and Social Psychology, 22*(1), 51–66. https://doi.org/10.1037/h0032356

Kahneman, D., & Tversky, A. (1979). Prospect theory: An analysis of decision under risk. *Econometrica, 47*(2), 263–291. https://doi.org/10.2307/1914185

Kapur, M. (2016). Examining productive failure, productive success, unproductive failure, and unproductive success in learning. *Educational Psychologist, 51*(2), 289–299. https://doi.org/10.1080/00461520.2016.1155457

Karwowski, M., & Beghetto, R. A. (2019). Creative behavior as agentic action. *Psychology of Aesthetics, Creativity, and the Arts, 13*(4), 402–415. https://doi.org/10.1037/aca0000190

Karwowski, M., Han, M.-H., & Beghetto, R. A. (2019). Toward dynamizing the measurement of creative confidence beliefs. *Psychology of Aesthetics, Creativity, and the Arts, 13*(2), 193–202. https://doi.org/10.1037/aca0000229

Karwowski, M., & Kaufman, J. C. (Eds.). (2017). *The Creative Self: Effect of Beliefs, Self-Efficacy, Mindset, and Identity*. Cambridge, MA: Academic Press.

Kaufman, J. C. (2016). *Creativity 101*. Cham: Springer.

Kaufman, J. C., & Beghetto, R. A. (2013). In praise of Clark Kent: Creative metacognition and the importance of teaching kids when (not) to be creative. *Roeper Review, 35*(3), 155–165.

Klein, G. (2007). Performing a project premortem. *Harvard Business Review, 85*, 18–19.

Kruglanski, A. W. (1990). Motivations for judging and knowing: Implications for causal attribution. In E. T. Higgins & R. M. Sorrentino (Eds.), *Handbook of Motivation and Cognition: Foundations of Social Behavior* (vol. 2, pp. 333–368). New York: The Guilford Press.

Lash, J. P. (1997). *Helen and Teacher: The Story of Helen Keller and Anne Sullivan Macy*. Cambridge, MA: Perseus Books.

Lavin, I. (1993). Picasso's Bull(s): Art history in reverse. *Art in America, 81*, 76–123.

Littleton, K., & Mercer, N. (2013). *Interthinking: Putting Talk to Work*. Abingdon: Routledge. https://doi.org/10.4324/9780203809433

Lord, C. G., Lepper, M. R., & Preston, E. (1984). Considering the opposite: A corrective strategy for social judgment. *Journal of Personality and Social Psychology, 47*(6), 1231–1243. https://doi.org/10.1037/0022-3514.47.6.1231

Manalo, E., & Kapur, M. (2018). The role of failure in promoting thinking skills and creativity: New findings and insights about how failure can be beneficial for learning. *Thinking Skills and Creativity, 30,* 1–6. https://doi.org/10.1016/j.tsc.2018.06.001

Mary Lou Fulton Teachers College (MLFTC). (2023). Principled innovation. https://pi.education.asu.edu

Masicampo, E. J., & Baumeister, R. F. (2012). Committed but closed-minded: When making a specific plan for a goal hinders success. *Social Cognition, 30,* 37–55. https://doi.org/10.1521/soco.2012.30.1.37

Matusov, E. (2009). *Journey into Dialogic Pedagogy.* Hauppauge, NY: Nova.

McCrae, R. R. (1987). Creativity, divergent thinking, and openness to experience. *Journal of Personality and Social Psychology, 52*(6), 1258–1265. https://doi.org/10.1037/0022-3514.52.6.1258

McDiarmid, G. W., & Zhao, Y. (2022). *Learning for Uncertainty: Teaching Students How to Thrive in a Rapidly Evolving World.* New York: Routledge.

Moran, S., & John-Steiner, V. (2004). How collaboration in creative work impacts identity and motivation. In D. Miell & K. Littleton (Eds.), *Collaborative Creativity: Contemporary Perspectives* (pp. 11–25). London: Free Association Books.

Mueller, J. S., Melwani, S., & Goncalo, J. A. (2012). The bias against creativity: Why people desire but reject creative ideas. *Psychological Science, 23,* 13–17.

Mumford, M. D., Mobley, M. I., Reiter-Palmon, R., Uhlman, C. E., & Doares, L. M. (1991). Process analytic models of creative capacities. *Creativity Research Journal, 4*(2), 91–122.

National Center for Education Statistics. (2022). Annual earnings by educational attainment. *Condition of Education.* U.S. Department of Education, Institute of Education Sciences. https://nces.ed.gov/programs/coe/indicator/cba

Nations Report Card. (2018). Technology and Engineering Literacy, 'Percentage of students assessed in eighth-grade NAEP technology and engineering literacy (TEL), by type of school and designing/creating to solve a problem.' www.nationsreportcard.gov/dashboards/schools_dashboard.aspx

Nickerson, J. A., Silverman, B. S., & Zenger, T. R. (2007). The "problem" of creating and capturing value. *Strategic Organization, 5*(3), 211–225. https://doi.org/10.1177/1476127007079969

Niu, W., & Zhou, Z. (2010). Creativity in mathematics teaching: A Chinese perspective. In R. A. Beghetto & J. C. Kaufman (Eds.), *Nurturing Creativity in the Classroom* (pp. 270–288). New York: Cambridge University Press.

Norcross, J. C., Mrykalo, M. S., & Blagys, M. D. (2002). *Auld lang Syne*: Success predictors, change processes, and self-reported outcomes of New Year's resolvers and nonresolvers. *Journal of Clinical Psychology, 58,* 397–405. https://doi.org/10.1002/jclp.1151

OECD. (2019). OECD Future of Education and Skills 2030: OECD LEARNING COMPASS 2030. www.oecd.org/education/2030-project/teaching-and-learning/learning/learning-compass-2030/OECD_Learning_Compass_2030_Concept_Note_Series.pdf

Oscarsson, M., Carlbring, P., Andersson, G., & Rozental, A. (2020). A large-scale experiment on New Year's resolutions: Approach-oriented goals are more successful than avoidance-oriented goals. *PLoS One, 15*. https://doi.org/10.1371/journal.pone.0234097

Pearson, P. David. (2004). "The reading wars." *Educational Policy, 18*(1), 216–252.

Peirce, C. S. (1958). *Collected Papers of Charles Sanders Peirce*. Vols. 5–8 A. W. Burks (Ed.). Cambridge, MA: Belknap Press of Harvard University Press.

Poli, R. (2020). *Handbook of Anticipation: Theoretical and Applied Aspects of the Use of Future in Decision Making*. Cham: Springer.

Pólya, G. (1966). On teaching problem solving. In *Conference Board of the Mathematical Sciences. The Role of Axiomatics and Problem Solving in Mathematics* (pp. 123–129). Boston: Ginn.

Ranciere, J. (1991). *The Ignorant Schoolmaster. Five Lessons in Intellectual Emancipation*. Translated and with an introduction by Kristin Ross. Stanford, CA: Stanford University Press.

Reece, A. G., Eubanks, A. D., Liebscher, A., & Baumeister, R. (2022, May 16). Enforcing pragmatic future-mindedness cures the innovator's bias. *Journal of Applied Social Psychology*. https://doi.org/10.1111/jasp.12956

Reeve, J. (2009). Why teachers adopt a controlling motivating style toward students and how they can become more autonomy supportive. *Educational Psychologist, 44*, 159–175.

Renzulli, J. S., Beghetto, R. A., Brandon, L. E., & Karwowski, M. (2022). Development of an instrument to measure opportunities for imagination, creativity, and innovation (ICI) in schools. *Gifted Education International, 38*(2), 174–193. www.doi.org/10.1177/02614294211042333

Roberts, B. W., Wood, D., & Caspi, A. (2008). The development of personality traits in adulthood. In O. P. John, R. W. Robins, & L. A. Pervin (Eds.), *Handbook of Personality: Theory and Research* (3rd ed., pp. 375–389). New York: Guilford Press.

Robertson, S. I. (2017). *Problem Solving* (2nd ed.). Abingdon: Routledge.

Roets, A., Kruglanski, A. W., Kossowska, M., Pierro, A., & Hong, Y. Y. (2015). The motivated gatekeeper of our minds: New directions in need for closure theory and research. In Mark P. Zanna & James M. Olson (Eds.), *Advances in Experimental Social Psychology* (vol. 52, pp. 221–283). Cambridge, MA: Academic Press.

Rothenberg, A. (1996). The Janusian process in scientific creativity. *Creativity Research Journal, 9*(2–3), 207–231. https://doi.org/10.1080/10400419.1996.9651173

Runco, M. A., & Acar, S. (2019). Divergent thinking. In J. C. Kaufman & R. J. Sternberg (Eds.), *The Cambridge Handbook of Creativity* (pp. 224–254). Cambridge: Cambridge University Press. https://doi.org/10.1017/9781316979839.013

Runco, M. A., & Chand, I. (1994). Problem finding, evaluative thinking, and creativity. In M. A. Runco (Ed.), *Problem Finding, Problem Solving, and Creativity* (pp. 40–76). Norwood, NJ: Ablex Publishing.

Sawyer, R. K. (2011). *Structure and Improvisation in Creative Teaching*. New York: Cambridge University Press.

(2012). *Explaining Creativity: The Science of Human Innovation*. Oxford: Oxford University Press.

(2013). *Zig Zag: The Surprising Path to Greater Creativity*. San Francisco: John Wiley & Sons.

Schwaba, T., Luhmann, M., Denissen, J. J. A., Chung, J. M., & Bleidorn, W. (2018). Openness to experience and culture-openness transactions across the lifespan. *Journal of Personality and Social Psychology*, *115*, 118–136. https://doi.org/10.1037/pspp0000150

Seligman, M. E. P., Railton, P., Baumeister, R. F., & Sripada, C. (2013). Navigating into the future or driven by the past. *Perspectives on Psychological Science*, *8*(2), 119–141. https://doi.org/10.1177/1745691612474317

Silvia, P. J. (2008). Discernment and creativity: How well can people identify their most creative ideas? *Psychology of Aesthetics, Creativity, and the Arts*, *2*(3), 139. https://doi.org/10.1037/1931-3896.2.3.139

Simonton, D. (2003). Creativity as variation and selection: Some critical constraints. In M. A. Runco (Ed.), *Critical Creative Processes* (pp. 3–18). Cresskill, NJ: Hampton Press.

Sirotnik, K. A. (1983). What you see is what you get: Consistency, persistency, and mediocrity in classrooms. *Harvard Educational Review*, *53*, 16–31.

Skidmore, D. (2000). From pedagogical dialogue to dialogical pedagogy. *Language and Education*, *14*(4), 283–296.

Snowling, M. J., & Hulme, C. (Eds.). (2005). *The Science of Reading: A Handbook*. Oxford: Blackwell.

Society for Science. (2022). '14-year-old develops robotic hand to help with disaster recovery; Wins $25,000 top award at the Broadcom MASTERS' www.prnewswire.com/news-releases/14-year-old-develops-robotic-hand-to-help-with-disaster-recovery-wins-25-000-top-award-at-the-broadcom-masters-301665640.html

Sparkman, D. J., Eidelman, S., & Blanchar, J. C. (2016). Multicultural experiences reduce prejudice through personality shifts in openness to experience. *European Journal of Social Psychology*, *46*, 840–853. https://doi.org/10.1002/ejsp.2189

Srinivasan, B. (2022). The network state: How to start a new country. https://thenetworkstate.com

Sternberg, R. J. (2021). Transformational creativity: The link between creativity, wisdom, and the solution of global problems. *Philosophies*, *6*, 75. https://doi.org/10.3390/philosophies6030075

Sternberg, R. J., Ambrose, D., & Karami, S. (Eds.). (2022). *The Palgrave Handbook of Transformational Giftedness for Education*. Cham: Palgrave Macmillan.

Sternberg, R. J., & Chowkase, A. (2021). When we teach for positive creativity, what exactly do we teach for? *Education Sciences*, *11*(5), 237.

Studer, J., Daly, S., McKilligan, S., & Seifert, C. (2018). Evidence of problem exploration in creative designs. *AI EDAM*, *32*(4), 415–430. https://doi.org/10.1017/S0890060418000124

The Youth Assembly (TYA). 2021. Outstanding youth delegate: Natalie Hampton. The Youth Assembly. www.youthassembly.org/2021/09/21/natalie-hampton/

Tiedens, L. Z., & Linton, S. (2001). Judgment under emotional certainty and uncertainty: The effects of specific emotions on information processing. *Journal of Personality and Social Psychology, 81*(6), 973–988.

Trope, Y., & Liberman, N. (2010). Construal-level theory of psychological distance. *Psychological Review, 117*, 440–463. https://doi.org/10.1037/a0018963

Tyack, D., & Tobin, W. (1994). The "grammar" of schooling: Why has it been so hard to change? *American Educational Research Journal, 31*(3), 453–479.

van Broekhoven, K., Belfi, B., Borghans, L., & Seegers, P. (2022). Creative idea forecasting: The effect of task exposure on idea evaluation. *Psychology of Aesthetics, Creativity, and the Arts, 16*(3), 519–528. https://doi.org/10.1037/aca0000426

Veinott, B., Klein, G. A., & Wiggins, S. (2010). Evaluating the effectiveness of the premortem technique on plan confidence. https://idl.iscram.org/files/veinott/2010/1049_Veinott_etal2010.pdf

Vyas, D., Heylen, D., Nijholt, A., & Van Der Veer, G. (2009). Collaborative practices that support creativity in design. In *ECSCW 2009* (pp. 151–170). London: Springer.

Vygotsky, L. S., & Cole, M. (1978). *Mind in Society: Development of Higher Psychological Processes*. Cambridge, MA: Harvard University Press.

Wagoner, B. (2008). Commentary: Making the familiar unfamiliar. *Culture & Psychology, 14*(4), 467–474. https://doi.org/10.1177/1354067X08096511

Ward, T., & Kolomyts, Y. (2019). Creative cognition. In J. Kaufman & R. Sternberg (Eds.), *The Cambridge Handbook of Creativity* (Cambridge Handbooks in Psychology, pp. 175–199). Cambridge: Cambridge University Press. https://doi.org/10.1017/9781316979839.011

Wiggins, G., & McTighe, J. (1998). *Understanding by Design*. Alexandria, VA: Association for Supervision and Curriculum Development.

Zenasni, F., Besançon, M., & Lubart, T. (2008). Creativity and tolerance of ambiguity: An empirical study. *The Journal of Creative Behavior, 42*(1), 61–73.

Zhao, Y. (2017). What works may hurt: Side effects in education. *Journal of Educational Change, 18*(1), 1–19.

Zhu, Y., Ritter, S. M., & Dijksterhuis, A. (2019). Creativity: Intrapersonal and interpersonal selection of creative ideas. *The Journal of Creative Behavior, 54*(3), 626–635. https://doi.org/10.1002/jocb.397

Zielińska, A., & Karwowski, M. (2022). Living with uncertainty in the creative process: A self-regulatory perspective. In R. A. Beghetto & G. J. Jaeger (Eds.), *Uncertainty: A Catalyst for Creativity, Learning and Development* (pp. 81–102). Cham: Springer. https://doi.org/10.1007/978-3-030-98729-9_6

Index

actionable possibilities, xiv, 8, 12, 17, 89, 96, 99, 100, 101, 102, 104, 105, 108, 109, 141
actionable uncertainty, 116, 117, 119
agentic beliefs, 120, 122, 125, 128, 129, 130
AI chatbots, xiv, 12
approach orientation, 56
artificial intelligence, xiii, 15, 16
"as if", 102, 152, 154
avoidance orientation, 56

backward design, 21, 22, 23, 26, 32, 49, 51
black swans, 7
blended designs, 49, 50
blended possibilities, 106
both/and approach, 39, 47
business-as-usual, 23, 30

Challenger Space Shuttle, 151
Cone of Contributions, 143
confidence, 4, 120, 131, 133, 135
contributions to future audiences, 148
contributions to immediate audiences, 145
contributions to oneself, 143
convergent thinking, 103
Creative Behavior as Agentic Action, 121
creative learning, 27, 28, 45, 139, 140, 141
creative sensemaking, 141
critical uncertainties, 60, 61

divergent thinking, 99, 103, 106

embracing uncertainty, xi, 29, 32, 37, 39
emergent outcomes, 77
everyday uncertainties, 60
expectancy x value, 123
exploration of the possible, 56, 57
exploratory mindset, 97, 98

failure, 47, 70, 113, 124, 125, 127, 128, 130, 151
forethought strategies, 129

forward design, 43
futures consciousness, 47

genuine doubt, 55
GPT model, xiii, 12, 37, 126, 131

hybrid lessons, 79, 82, 83, 85, 90

"if not-then" thinking, 153
Imagination, Creativity, and Innovation (ICI) index, 42
impact to broader community, 146
impending uncertainties, 60, 62
indefinite stability, 55, 59
innovator bias, 107, 151, 152
IRE, 24, 29, 32, 33, 34, 36

known-knowns, 15, 21, 22, 26, 30, 34, 43, 45, 46, 47, 49, 50, 89, 147
known-unknowns, 43, 45, 49

legacy projects, 84
lesson unplanning, 80
likely futures, xiv, 6, 7, 10, 11, 20, 21, 23, 31, 40, 43, 45
logic of backward design, 21, 23, 26, 29, 30, 32, 34, 40, 49

make the familiar unfamiliar, 100
make the unfamiliar familiar, 100
metaphysical uncertainties, 60, 63
multiple futures, 5

need for closure, 57
non-routine problems, 45, 80

Openai's playground, xiii, 126
openness to experience, 98

performance strategies, 129
possibility thinking, xi, xiii, 9, 10, 59, 96, 108, 111, 152, 154, 160
pragmatic pretense, 8, 9
pre-test, 107, 109, 141
principled approach, xiv–xv, 150, 152, 154, 155
problem exploration, 97, 98
problem finding, 84
prototypical design, 20, 21
psychological distance, 8

resolve uncertainty, 32, 40, 48, 57, 59, 84, 97, 120, 121, 122, 125

scenarios, xi, 7, 8, 9, 10, 12, 13, 15, 40, 53, 114
selecting possibilities, 103
self-reflection strategies, 130
self-regulation, 128
setbacks, 47, 87, 111, 113, 125, 127, 128, 130, 135, 142, 143, 153, 154
social support, 116, 118, 122, 125, 127, 128, 140
structured uncertainty, 45, 77, 79, 80, 81, 82, 83, 89, 161
student loan debt crisis, 29
suspended conclusion, 57

teacher and student knowing and unknowing, 64
thresholds of action, 116, 117
"top two" approach, 105
transactional, 3, 29, 30, 48, 88, 124, 143
transformational learning, 28, 46, 48, 50, 53

uncertain futures, 6, 7, 19, 20, 41, 43, 45, 50, 52
unknown futures, xiv, 6, 7, 10, 11, 19, 26, 30, 46, 48, 62, 78
unknown-unknowns, 7
UxD, xiv–xv, 31, 43, 44, 45, 46, 47, 49, 50, 51, 52, 53, 55, 58, 60, 62, 63, 64, 66, 67, 68, 71, 77, 79, 80, 83, 84, 85, 86, 87, 88, 90, 93, 94, 95, 96, 97, 98, 99, 100, 103, 105, 106, 108, 116, 118, 119, 120, 121, 122, 123, 124, 125, 126, 127, 128, 129, 130, 131, 133, 135, 137, 139, 140, 141, 142, 143, 145, 146, 147, 148, 149, 150, 151, 152, 153, 154, 155, 156, 160, 161

"what if", 152, 154
"what if-not" thinking, 152
wildcard, 6, 8, 14, 17

zone of proximal development, 118

Milton Keynes UK
Ingram Content Group UK Ltd.
UKHW040158011224
451573UK00012B/135